PUBLISHER'S NOTE TO THE SECOND EDITION

We are happy to say that this second edition of the *Kaṭha Upaniṣad* has been thoroughly revised by the translator himself.

Mayavati PUBLISHER

10 October 1987

PUBLISHER'S NOTE TO THE FIRST EDITION

The *Kaṭha Upaniṣad* is the penultimate to be published in the present series, each Upaniṣad being taken out in its entirety from the author's well-known *Eight Upaniṣads* in two volumes published by us. The remaining one is the *Taittirīya*.

In the translation of the commentary, the words quoted from the text by Śaṅkarācārya, are given in italics. These are followed by commas and the English equivalents. Informative explanatory footnotes have been added wherever necessary.

This Upaniṣad forms a part of the Brāhmaṇa belonging to the Kaṭha Śākhā of the *Kṛṣṇa Yajur-Veda*. The *Kaṭha Upaniṣad* stands in a class by itself. It combines charming poetry, elevating mysticism, and profound philosophy. The subject of the mystery of death is introduced through the medium of an interesting anecdote; and the teaching of the Upaniṣad is presented in the form of a dialogue between young Naciketā, a mere boy (कुमार), who had gone to the abode of Yama, the King of Death, in search of the mystery underlying the life and death of mortals. Naciketā is the student, the seeker, and Yama, the teacher, than whom there could be none better to impart the knowledge sought by the young student. In the course of the dialogue between them, there issues forth from the lips of Yama the wisdom that lies beyond life and death: an exposition of the nature of the Self, the intimate spiritual essence of our being as well as the ultimate Reality of all exist-

KAṬHA UPANIṢAD

With the Commentary of

ŚAṄKARĀCĀRYA

Translated by

Swami Gambhirananda

Advaita Ashrama
(Publication Department)
5 Dehi Entally Road
Kolkata 700 014

Published by
Swami Mumukshananda
President, Advaita Ashrama
Mayavati, Champawat, Himalayas
from its Publication Department, Kolkata
Email : advaita@vsnl.com
Website : www.advaitaonline.com

Sixth Impression, May 2004
3M3C

ISBN 81-85301-33-6

Printed in India at
Trio Process
Kolkata 700 014

ence, in an unambiguous language. It also points to the limitations of logical reason and the inadequacy of mere scriptural scholarship in realizing this deepest core of the reality imbedded in the heart of every being.

Swami Vivekananda, that paramount protagonist of the Upaniṣads in recent times, was greatly fascinated by this Upaniṣad. He goes into ecstasy whenever he refers to the *śraddhā* of Naciketā and of his sterling character. The Swami devotes two entire lectures in his *Jñāna-yoga* to an exposition of this Upaniṣad. His repeated and most popular exhortation, 'Arise! Awake! And stop not till the goal is reached', is based on one of the verses of this Upaniṣad, the latter part of which warns the seeker to be wary on his path, compared to the sharp edge of a razor (क्षुरस्य धारा निशिता), which is difficult to cross and hard to tread. The Upaniṣad proclaims in unmistakable terms that intuitional perception of the Ātman cannot be had by the unrestrained, unmeditative, and unpacified mind. Here occurs that very instructive imagery of the human body compared to a chariot, with its full complements of the master of the chariot (the soul), the charioteer (the intellect), the rein (the mind), the horses (the senses), and their roads (the sense-objects).

It is with great pleasure that we place this edition of the *Kaṭha Upaniṣad* in the hands of the earnest seekers after truth and lovers of spiritual knowledge.

PUBLISHER

Mayavati
10 February 1980

CONTENTS

KEY TO TRANSLITERATION AND PRONUNCIATION

		Sounds like
अ	a	o in s*o*n
आ	ā	a in m*a*ster
इ	i	i in *i*f
ई	ī	ee in f*ee*l
उ	u	u in f*u*ll
ऊ	ū	oo in b*oo*t
ऋ	ṛ	somewhat between r and ri
ए	e	a in ev*a*de
ऐ	ai	y in m*y*
ओ	o	o in *o*ver
औ	au	ow in n*ow*
क	k	k
ख	kh	ckh in blo*ckh*ead
ग	g	g (hard)
घ	gh	gh in lo*g-h*ut
ङ	ṅ	ng
च	c	ch (not k)
छ	ch	chh in cat*ch h*im
ज	j	j
झ	jh	dgeh in he*dgeh*og
ञ	ñ	n (somewhat)
ट	ṭ	t
ठ	ṭh	th in an*t-h*ill

		Sounds like
ड	ḍ	d
ढ	ḍh	dh in go*dh*ood
ण	ṇ	n in u*n*der
त	t	French t
थ	th	th in *th*umb
द	d	th in *th*en
ध	dh	theh in brea*the h*ere
न	n	n
प	p	p
फ	ph	ph in loo*p-h*ole
ब	b	b
भ	bh	bh in a*bh*or
म	m	m
य	y	y
र	r	r
ल	l	l
व	v	v in a*v*ert
श	ś	sh
ष	ṣ	sh in *sh*ow
स	s	s
ह	h	h
.	ṁ	m in hu*m*
:	ḥ	half h in hu*h*!

LIST OF ABBREVIATIONS

A. G.	...	Ānanda Giri
Ai.	...	Aitareya Upaniṣad
Bṛ.	...	Bṛhadāraṇyaka Upaniṣad
Ch.	...	Chāndogya Upaniṣad
Cit.	...	Cityupaniṣad
G.	...	Bhagavad Gītā
Iti.	...	Itihāsa Upaniṣad
L. P.	...	Liṅga Purāṇa
Mu.	...	Muṇḍaka Upaniṣad
Ṛ.	...	Ṛg-Veda
Śve.	...	Śvetāśvatara Upaniṣad
Tai.	...	Taittirīya Upaniṣad
V. P.	...	Viṣṇu Purāṇa

KAṬHA UPANIṢAD

ॐ सह नाववतु। सह नौ भुनक्तु। सह वीर्यं करवावहै।
तेजस्वि नावधीतमस्तु। मा विद्विषावहै॥

ॐ शान्तिः शान्तिः शान्तिः॥

May He protect us both (the teacher and the taught) together (by revealing knowledge). May He protect us both (by vouchsafing the results of knowledge). May we attain vigour together. Let what we study be invigorating. May we not cavil at each other.

Om ! Peace ! Peace ! Peace !

KATHA UPANIṢAD

PART I

Canto I

Introduction: Salutation to Bhagavān[1] Yama (Death), son of the Sun and the imparter of the knowledge of Brahman, and salutation to Naciketā.

Now then, a brief exposition of the cantos of the Kaṭha Upaniṣad is begun for the sake of making their import easily comprehensible. The word *upaniṣad* is derived by adding *upa* (near) and *ni* (with certainty) as prefixes and *kvip* as a suffix to the root *sad*, meaning to split up (destroy), go (reach, attain), or loosen. And by the word *upaniṣad* is denoted the knowledge of the knowable entity presented in the book that is going to be explained. By virtue of what relation with (any particular) significance (of the word *upaniṣad*), again, is knowledge denoted by the word *upaniṣad*? This is being stated. Knowledge is called *upaniṣad* by virtue of its association with this significance: It (viz knowledge) splits up, injures, or destroys the seeds of worldly existence such as ignorance etc., in the case of those seekers of emancipation who, after becoming detached from the desire for the seen and unseen[2] objects, approach (*upa sad*) the knowl-

[1] One who has knowledge of creation and dissolution (of the worlds), of birth and death of creatures, and of ignorance and knowledge.

[2] *Ānuśravika* (unseen objects) 'revealed in the scriptures (Vedas), such as enjoyment in heaven etc.'—A.G.

edge that is called *upaniṣad* and that bears the characteristics to be presented hereafter, and who then deliberate on it with steadiness and certainty (*ni*).[1] Thus it will be said later on, 'knowing That, one becomes freed from the jaws of Death' (I. iii. 15). Or the knowledge of Brahman is called *upaniṣad* because of its connection with the idea of leading to Brahman, inasmuch as it makes the seekers after emancipation, who are possessed of the qualities already mentioned, attain the supreme Brahman. Thus it will be said later on, 'Having become free from virtue and vice, as also desire and ignorance, (he) attained Brahman' (II. iii. 18). And even the knowledge about Fire, who preceded all the worlds, who was born of Brahmā and is possessed of enlightenment, and whose knowledge is prayed for (by Naciketā) through the second boon (I. i. 13), is also called *upaniṣad* by virtue of its bearing the meaning (to loosen) of the root (*sad*), inasmuch as by leading to the result, achievement of heaven, it weakens or loosens such multitude of miseries as living in the womb, birth, old age, etc., continually recurring in lives hereafter. Thus it will be spoken, 'The dwellers of heaven get immortality', etc. (ibid).

Objection: Is it not a fact that by the word *upaniṣad* the readers refer to the book as well in such sentences as: 'We read the *upaniṣad*', and 'We teach the *upaniṣad*'?

[1] 'Approaching' means 'receiving through the instruction of the teacher', and 'deliberate' means 'eliminate the idea of impossibility etc. with regard to such things as the unity of the individual self and the transcendental Self.'—A.G.

Answer: Though, from this point of view, the meanings of the root *sad*—such as loosening the causes of the world, viz ignorance etc.—are inapplicable with regard to a mere book, and applicable to knowledge, still this is no fault, since the book, too, being meant for that purpose, can justifiably be denoted by that word, as for instance (in the sentence) 'Clarified butter is indeed life.' Therefore, with regard to knowledge, the word *upaniṣad* is used in its primary sense, while with regard to a book it is used in a secondary sense.

Thus, through the very derivation of the word *upaniṣad*, the person particularly qualified for knowledge has been pointed out. And the subject matter of the knowledge is also shown to be a unique thing, viz the supreme Brahman that is the indwelling Self. And the purpose of this *upaniṣad* is the absolute cessation of the transmigratory state, which consists in the attainment of Brahman.[1] And the connection (between knowledge and its purpose) has been mentioned *ipso facto* through the enunciation of such a purpose.[2] Thus these cantos themselves are (meant)

[1] Total cessation of the world (i.e. rotation of birth and death) follows the eradication of ignorance. And since the non-existence of a superimposed thing is identical with the thing on which the superimposition occurs, the cessation of the world is the same as the attainment of Brahman. Or *brahmaprāptilakṣaṇā* in the commentary may mean that the cessation (of the world) is indicative of the realization of the supreme Bliss that is Brahman.

[2] 'Knowledge is needed for the removal of ignorance which cannot be eradicated through work. So the goal of knowledge is connected with itself, as an end is with its means.'—A.G.

for special persons (competent for their study), and have a special subject matter, a special purpose, and a special connection, inasmuch as they reveal, like an apple (lit. emblic myrobalan) placed in the hand, the knowledge that is (meant) for a man of special competence, and has a special subject matter, a special purpose, and a special connection as already explained. Hence we shall explain these cantos to the best of our understanding. The story there is by way of eulogizing the knowledge.

ॐ उशन् ह वै वाजश्रवसः सर्ववेदसं ददौ ।
तस्य ह नचिकेता नाम पुत्र आस ॥१॥

1. Once upon a time, the son of Vājaśravā, being desirous of fruit, gave away everything. He had, as the story goes, a son named Naciketā.

Uśan, being desirous of; *ha* and *vai* (equivalent to—once upon a time) are two indeclinable particles, recalling to mind what happened before. Vājaśravā is he whose *śravaḥ*, fame, is consequent on the giving of *vājam*, food. Or it is a proper name. His son, Vājaśravasa, being desirous of the fruit of the sacrifice, performed the *Viśvajit* sacrifice in which all is given away. In that sacrifice, he *dadau*, gave away; *sarvavedasam*, all (his) wealth. *Tasya*, of him, of that performer of sacrifice; *āsa*, there was; *ha*, as the story goes; *naciketā nāma putraḥ*, a son named Naciketā.

तꣳ ह कुमारꣳ सन्तं दक्षिणासु नीयमानासु श्रद्धाविवेश
सोऽमन्यत ॥२॥

2. As the presents were being carried (to the Brāhmaṇas) faith took possession of him who was still a boy. He thought:

Tam, into him, into Naciketā; *kumāraṁ santam*, while still in the prime of life, still not adolescent, still a mere boy; *śraddhā*, faith (in the verity of the scriptures), induced by a desire for his father's good; *āviveśa*, entered. At what time? This is being stated: *dakṣiṇāsu nīyamānāsu*, when gifts were being carried, when cows meant for presents were being led separately (according to each one's due), to the priests and the assembled Brāhmaṇas; *saḥ*, he, that Naciketā who had an influx of faith; *amanyata*, thought.

How he thought is being stated in *pītodakā* etc.

पीतोदका जग्धतृणा दुग्धदोहा निरिन्द्रियाः ।
अनन्दा नाम ते लोकास्तान् स गच्छति ता ददत् ॥३॥

3. He goes to those worlds that are known as joyless, who gives away the cows that have drunk water and eaten grass (for good), whose milk has been milked (for the last time), and which have lost their organs.

The cows meant for offering to the Brāhmaṇas are being described: Those by which *udakam*, water, has been *pītam*, drunk, are *pītodakāḥ*;[1] those by which

[1] 'Water has been drunk earlier only; but later on, even the power to drink water is absent. Similarly, there is no power to eat grass or give milk.'—A.G.

tṛṇam, grass, has been *jagdham*, eaten, are *jagdha-tṛṇāḥ*; those whose *dohaḥ*, milk, has been *dugdhaḥ*, milked, are *dugdha-dohāḥ*; *nirindriyāḥ*, those that are devoid of the power of their organs, incapable of bearing calves; that is to say, the cows that are decrepit and barren. *Dadat*, giving; *tāḥ*, those, the cows that are of this kind; to the priests as rewards for their service; *saḥ*, he, the performer of sacrifice; *gacchati*, goes; *tān*, to those (worlds); *anandāḥ nāma te lokāḥ*, which worlds are known as devoid of happiness, joyless.

स होवाच पितरं तत कस्मै मां दास्यसीति ।
द्वितीयं तृतीयं तꣳ होवाच मृत्यवे त्वा ददामीति ॥४॥

4. He said to his father, 'Father, to whom will you offer me?' He spoke to him a second time and a third time. To him (the father) said, 'To Death I offer you.'

'The evil result thus accruing to my father as a consequence of the imperfection of the sacrifice should be warded off by me, who am a good son, by perfecting the sacrifice even through an offering of myself', thinking thus, *saḥ*, he—approached his father; and *uvāca ha*, said; *pitaram*, to the father; '*Tata* (same as *tāta*), O father; *kasmai*, to whom, to which of the priests; *mām dāsyasi*, will you offer me, that is to say, offer me as a present?' *iti*. Though ignored by his father who was addressed thus, *dvitīyam tṛtīyam uvāca*, he spoke even a second time and a third time, thus: 'To whom will you offer me?' 'To whom will you offer me?' Incensed at the thought, 'This one is not behaving like a boy', the father *uvāca ha*, said; *tam*, to him, to his son; '*Mṛtyave*, to Death, to the son of the Sun; *dadāmi*, I give away; *tvā* (which is same as *tvām*), you'; *iti*, (this much).

That son, having been spoken to thus, sorrowfully cogitated in a solitary place. How? That is being said:

बहूनामेमि प्रथमो बहूनामेमि मध्यमः ।
किꣳ स्विद्यमस्य कर्तव्यं यन्मयाऽद्य करिष्यति ॥५॥

5. Among many I rank as belonging to the highest; among many I rank as belonging to the middling. What purpose can there be of Death that my father will get achieved today through me?

Bahūnām, among many—of many sons or disciples; *emi*, I go (rank); *prathamaḥ*, as first owing to the best conduct of a disciple etc. This is the idea. And *bahūnām*, among many—many middling ones; *madhyamaḥ emi*, I move (count) as a middling one, I behave in a middling manner. But never do I behave as the worst.[1] Though I am a son possessed of such quality, still to me my father has said, 'To Death I offer you.' *Kim svit*, what; *kartavyam*, purpose; *yamasya*, of Death—can there be; which purpose he (my father) *adya*, today; *kariṣyati*, will achieve; *mayā*, through me, by sending me?

[1] 'The best conduct consists in engaging in the service of the teacher by ascertaining his wishes at the proper time. Acting on command is middling conduct. And disobedience to such orders is the worst.'—A.G.

'My father must have certainly spoken so out of anger, without any consideration of purpose. Still, that utterance of the father must not be falsified', thinking thus, he said sorrowfully to his father, remorseful as the latter was because of the thought 'What a thing I have uttered!'

अनुपश्य यथा पूर्वे प्रतिपश्य तथाऽपरे ।
सस्यमिव मर्त्यः पच्यते सस्यमिवाजायते पुनः ॥६॥

6. Consider successively how your forefathers behaved, and consider how others behave (now). Man decays and dies like corn, and emerges again like corn.

Anupaśya: *anu*, successively; *paśya*, consider, have a look at; *yathā*, how; your, *pūrve*, forebears, dead father, grandfather and others behaved. And seeing them, it behoves you to tread in their footsteps. *Tathā*, similarly too; as *apare*, others—other holy men behave; them also you *pratipaśya*, consider. Not that in them there ever was, or is, any falsification. Opposed to that is the behaviour of bad people, which consists of paltering with truth. Besides, not by prevarication can anyone become free from death and decrepitude. For *martyaḥ*, man; *sasyam iva*, like corn; *pacyate*, decays and dies; and after dying, *punaḥ*, again; *sasyam iva ājāyate*, reappears (is born) like corn. Thus what does one gain in this impermanent human world by breaking one's own words? Protect your own truth, and send me to Death. This is the idea.

Having been addressed thus, the father sent (him) for the sake of his own veracity. And he, having gone to Death's abode, lived for three nights (i.e. days), Death being out. When Death returned from his sojourn, his councillors or wives said to him by way of advice:

वैश्वानरः प्रविशत्यतिथिर्ब्राह्मणो गृहान् ।
तस्यैताꣳ शान्तिं कुर्वन्ति हर वैवस्वतोदकम् ॥७॥

7. A Brāhmaṇa guest enters the houses like fire. For him they accomplish this kind of propitiation. O Death, carry water (for him).

Brāhmaṇaḥ, a Brāhmaṇa; as *atithiḥ*, a guest; *praviśati*, enters; like *vaiśvānaraḥ*, fire itself; as though burning *gṛhān*, the houses. Since *tasya*, for his sake—for the guest; the good people *kurvanti*, accomplish; *etām*, this kind of; *śāntim*, propitiation —consisting in offering water for washing feet, a seat, etc., just as people do for allaying the conflagration of fire—and since evil consequences are declared in case of not doing so (Mu. I. ii. 3); therefore *vaivasvata*, O Death; *hara*, carry; *udakam*, water —for Naciketā, for washing his feet.

आशाप्रतीक्षे संगतꣳ सूनृतां
इष्टापूर्ते पुत्रपशूꣳश्च सर्वान् ।
एतद्वृङ्क्ते पुरुषस्याल्पमेधसो
यस्यानश्नन्वसति ब्राह्मणो गृहे ॥८॥

8. If in anyone's house a Brāhmaṇa guest abides

without food, that Brāhmaṇa destroys hope and expectation, the results of holy association and sweet discourse, sacrifices and charities, sons and cattle—all these—of that man of little intelligence.

Āśāpratīkṣe: *āśā* is the wish for a desirable thing which is attainable though unknown; *pratīkṣā* is expectation for something that is attainable and known; these two, hope and expectation, are *āśāpratīkṣe*; *saṁgatam* is the fruit derived from the association with the holy people[1]; *sūnṛtām ca*: *sūnṛtā* is sweet discourse—the fruit of that also; *iṣṭā-pūrte*: *iṣṭa* is the fruit of sacrifice and *pūrta* is that of (charitable) work like construction of rest-houses etc.; *putra-paśūn ca*, sons and cattle; *sarvān etat* should be *sarvam etat*, all this, as described; (he) *vṛṅkte*, excludes (from), i.e. destroys; *purusasya alpamedhasaḥ*, from (i.e. of) a man of little intelligence; *yasya*, in whose; *gṛhe*, house; *brāhmaṇaḥ*, a Brāhmaṇa; *vasati*, abides; *anaśnan*, without food. Therefore, a guest should not be neglected under any condition. This is the idea.

Having been told thus, Death approached Naciketā with adoration and said:

तिस्रो रात्रीर्यदवात्सीर्गृहे मे
अनश्नन् ब्रह्मन्नतिथिर्नमस्यः ।

[1] We read this portion of the commentary as '*saṁgatam, sat-saṁyogajam*'. But some read it as '*saṁgatam, tatsaṁyogajam*', which means 'the fruit resulting from association with that, viz the objects of hope and expectation'.

नमस्तेऽस्तु ब्रह्मन् स्वस्ति मेऽस्तु
तस्मात्प्रति त्रीन्वरान्वृणीष्व ॥९॥

9. O Brāhmaṇa, since you have lived in my house for three nights without food, a guest and an adorable person as you are, let my salutations be to you, and let good accrue to me (by averting the fault arising) from that (lapse). Ask for three boons—one in respect of each (night).

Brahman, O Brāhmaṇa; *yat*, since; *avātsīḥ*, you have lived; *gṛhe me*, in my house; *tisraḥ rātrīḥ*, for three nights; *anaśnan*, without eating; *atithiḥ*, a guest; and *namasyaḥ*, worthy of being saluted (venerable)—as you are; therefore *namaḥ te astu*, let salutations be to you. *Brahman*, O Brāhmaṇa; let there be *svasti*, good fortune; *me*, for me; through the aversion of the evil accruing *tasmāt*, therefrom, from the lapse caused by your abiding in my house without food. Although all good will befall me through your favour, still for your propitiation all the more, *vṛṇīṣva*, ask for: *trīn varān*, three boons—any particular three things you like; *prati*, one in respect of—each night you have spent without food.

As for Naciketā, he said:

शान्तसंकल्पः सुमना यथा स्या-
द्वीतमन्युर्गौतमो माऽभि मृत्यो ।
त्वत्प्रसृष्टं माऽभिवदेत्प्रतीत
एतत् त्रयाणां प्रथमं वरं वृणे ॥१०॥

10. O Death, of the three boons I ask this one as the first, viz that (my father) Gautama may become freed from anxiety, calm of mind, freed from anger towards me, and he may recognize me and talk to me when freed by you.

If you want to grant boons, then, *mṛtyo*, O Death; (I pray so) *yathā*, as my father *gautamaḥ*, Gautama; *syāt*, may become; *śānta-saṁkalpaḥ*—one whose mind is freed, with regard to me, from the anxiety, 'How may my son behave after reaching Death'; *sumanāḥ*, calm of mind; and also *vītamanyuḥ*, free from anger; *mā abhi*, towards me; moreover, he *abhivadet*, may talk to; *mā*, me; *tvatprasṛṣṭam*, freed by you—sent towards home; *pratītaḥ*, getting his memory revived, i. e. recognizing (me) thus: 'That very son of mine is come'[1]; *trayāṇām*, of the three boons; *vṛṇe*, I ask for; *prathamam*, as the first boon; *etat*, this one—that has this purpose, viz the satisfaction of my father.

Death said:

यथा पुरस्ताद् भविता प्रतीत
औद्दालकिरारुणिर्मत्प्रसृष्टः ।
सुखꣳ रात्रीः शयिता वीतमन्यु-
स्त्वां ददृशिवान्मृत्युमुखात् प्रमुक्तम् ॥११॥

[1] 'Favour me in such a way that my father may not avoid me under the idea, "This one has returned after becoming a ghost; he is not to be looked at." '—A.G.

11. Having recognized (you), Auddālaki Āruṇi will be (possessed of affection) just as he had before. Seeing you freed from the jaws of Death, he will get over his anger and will, with my permission, sleep happily for many a night.

Yathā, as—the kind of affectionate feeling that your father had towards you; *purastāt*, before; your father *auddālakiḥ*, Auddālaki; *pratītaḥ*, having recognized (you); *bhavitā*, will become—possessed of affection, in that very same way. Uddālaka and Auddālaki refer to the same (person). And he is *Āruṇiḥ*, the son of Aruṇa; or he bears two family names.[1] *Matprasṛṣṭaḥ*, being permitted by me; (your father) *śayitā*, will sleep; during *rātrīḥ*, nights—other (future) nights, too; *sukham*, happily—with a composed mind; and he will become *vītamanyuḥ* free from anger—as well; *tvām dadṛśivān*, having seen you—his son; *mṛtyumukhāt pramuktam*, as having been freed from the jaws—from the grasp—of Death.

Naciketā said:

स्वर्गे लोके न भयं किंचनास्ति
न तत्र त्वं न जरया बिभेति।

[1] The suffix in *auddālaki* may not add any meaning to the original word *uddālaka*, or it may signify the son of Uddālaka. In the latter case, he becomes a scion of the Uddālakas as also of the Aruṇas. This was possible when a brotherless girl was given in marriage with the stipulation that her son would be counted as belonging to either family, so that the offering of rice balls etc. to the departed of both the lines might be guaranteed.

उभे तीर्त्वाऽशनायापिपासे
शोकातिगो मोदते स्वर्गलोके ॥१२॥

12. In heaven there is no fear—you are not there, (and) nobody is struck with fear because of old age. Having transcended both hunger and thirst, and crossed over sorrow, one rejoices in the heavenly world.

Svarge loke, in the heavenly world; *bhayam kimcana na asti*, there is no fear whatsoever—fear arising from disease etc.; and *tvam*, you, O Death; *na tatra*, are not there—you do not exert your might there all of a sudden; so, unlike what happens in this world, there *jarayā*, because of old age; *na bibheti*, nobody shudders—at you. Moreover, *ubhe aśanāyā-pipāse tīrtvā*, having transcended both hunger and thirst; and *śokātigaḥ*, having crossed over sorrow—being free from mental unhappiness; (one) *modate*, rejoices; *svargaloke*, in the divine heavenly world.

स त्वमग्निꣳ स्वर्ग्यमध्येषि मृत्यो
प्रब्रूहि त्वꣳ श्रद्दधानाय मह्यम् ।
स्वर्गलोका अमृतत्वं भजन्त
एतद् द्वितीयेन वृणे वरेण ॥१३॥

13. O Death, such as you are, you know that Fire which leads to heaven. Of that you tell me who am full of faith. The dwellers of heaven get immortality. This I ask for through the second boon.

Mṛtyo, O Death; since *saḥ tvam*, you, such as you

are; *adhyeṣi*, remember, i.e. know; *svargyam agnim*, the Fire that is the means for the attainment of heaven—heaven that is possessed of the qualities aforesaid; (therefore) *tvam*, you; *prabrūhi*, speak; *mahyam śraddadhānāya*, to me who am full of faith, and who pray for heaven—(tell me of that Fire) by worshipping which; *svarga-lokāḥ*, the dwellers of heaven, those who have got heaven as their place of attainment, the sacrificers; *bhajante*, get; *amṛtatvam*, immortality, divinity. That fact which is *etat*, this knowledge of Fire; *vṛṇe*, I seek for; *dvitīyena vareṇa*, through the second boon.

This is the promise of Death:

प्र ते ब्रवीमि तदु मे निबोध
स्वर्ग्यमग्निं नचिकेतः प्रजानन् ।
अनन्तलोकाप्तिमथो प्रतिष्ठां
विद्धि त्वमेतं निहितं गुहायाम् ॥१४॥

14. O Naciketā, being well aware of the Fire that is conducive to heaven, I shall tell you of it. That very thing you understand, with attention, from my words. That Fire which is the means for the attainment of heaven and which is the support of the world, know it to be established in the intellect (of the enlightened ones).

Naciketaḥ, O Naciketā; *te*, to you; *pra-bravīmi*, I shall say—what was prayed for by you. *Me*, from me, from my words; *nibodha*, understand with attention; *tat u*, that very thing; viz *svargyam agnim*, the Fire that is conducive to heaven—that is the means for the attainment of heaven; which I shall tell you, *prajānan*, being well aware of (it)—this is the idea. The expressions, 'I shall tell you' and 'understand with attention' are meant for fixing the attention of the disciple (on the subject). Now he praises the Fire: That (Fire) which is *anantalokāptim*, the attainment of infinite world—that is, the means for the attainment of the result, viz heaven; *atho*, and also; *pratiṣṭhām*, the support—of the universe in the form of Virāṭ[1] (Cosmic Person). *Etam*, this, this Fire which is being spoken of by me; *viddhi*, you know; (as) *nihitam guhāyām*, located in the hidden place—i.e. placed in the intellect of men of knowledge.

These are words of the Upaniṣad itself:

लोकादिमग्निं तमुवाच तस्मै
    या इष्टका यावतीर्वा यथा वा।
स चापि तत्प्रत्यवदद्यथोक्त-
    मथास्य मृत्युः पुनरेवाह तुष्टः ॥१५॥

15. Death told him of the Fire that is the source of the world, the class and number of bricks, as also the manner of arranging for the fire. And he (Naci-

[1] 'In the Bṛhadāraṇyaka Upaniṣad we read: "He (Virāṭ—the Cosmic Person, embodied in the gross universe) differentiated himself in three ways" (I. ii. 3), from which Vedic text it follows that it is the cosmic Virāṭ who exists as fire, air and the sun. Fire as constituting that aspect of Virāṭ, is the support of the universe.' —A.G.

ketā), too, repeated verbatim, with understanding, all these as they were spoken. Then Death, being satisfied with this, said again:

Tasmai, to him, to Naciketā; Death *uvāca*, spoke of; *tam lokādim agnim*, that Fire—that is being dealt with, and that was prayed for by Naciketā—the Fire which (as Virāṭ) preceded the world—since it was the first embodied being. Moreover, *yāḥ iṣṭakāḥ*, the class of bricks, that are to be collected (for the sacrificial altar); *yāvatīḥ vā*, how many (the bricks are to be) in number; *yathā vā*, or how—how the fire is to be arranged[1]—all these he said, this is the significance. *Saḥ ca api*, and he, Naciketā, too; *pratyavadat*, repeated verbatim, with understanding; *tat*, all that; *yathoktam*, just as Death had spoken. *Atha*, then; *tuṣṭaḥ*, being satisfied, by his repition; *mṛtyuḥ*, Death; *punaḥ eva āha*, said over again—desiring to offer another boon besides the three.

तमब्रवीत् प्रीयमाणो महात्मा
वरं तवेहाद्य ददामि भूयः।
तवैव नाम्ना भविताऽयमग्निः
सृङ्कां चेमामनेकरूपां गृहाण ॥१६॥

16. Feeling delighted, that high-souled one said to him, 'Out of favour towards you, I now grant

[1] How the sacrificial wood is to be piled up, how the fire is to be procured, and how it is to be lit up.

again another boon. This fire will be known by your name indeed. And accept this multiformed necklace as well.

How did he say? *Prīyamāṇaḥ*, being delighted—feeling highly pleased at the fitness of the disciple; *mahātmā*, the high-souled one, one who was not narrow-minded; *tam*, to him, to Naciketā; *abravīt*, said: '*Iha*, here, out of favour; *tava*, towards you; a fourth boon,[1] *adya*, now; *dadāmi*, I offer; *bhūyaḥ*, again. *Ayam agniḥ*, this fire—the fire that is being spoken of by me; *bhavitā*, will become—famous; *tava eva nāmnā*, by your name indeed. *Ca*, moreover; *gṛhāṇa*, accept; *imām*, this; *sṛṅkām*, necklace; (which is) *anekarūpām*, multiformed and variegated—resounding, set with jewels, and of various hues. Or *sṛṅkām* (may mean) the course—that consists of rites and is not ignoble; *gṛhāṇa*, you accept.' The idea is this: 'You accept an additional knowledge about (variegated) *karma*—(multiformed) because it leads to various results.'

He (Yama) praises the *karma* itself again:

त्रिणाचिकेतस्त्रिभिरेत्य सन्धि
त्रिकर्मकृत्तरति जन्ममृत्यू ।
ब्रह्मजज्ञं देवमीडयं विदित्वा
निचाय्येमाꣳ शान्तिमत्यन्तमेति ॥१७॥

[1] The other three being, his father's composure, knowledge about Fire, and knowledge of the Self.

17. 'One who, getting connection with the three, piles up the Nāciketa fire thrice, and undertakes three kinds of work, crosses over death. Getting knowledge of that omniscient One who is born of Brahmā and is the praiseworthy Deity, and realizing Him, he attains this peace fully.

Sandhim etya, getting connection; *tribhiḥ*, with the three—with mother, father, and teacher, i.e. getting his instruction from mother etc., properly—for that is known as a source of valid knowledge from another Vedic text: 'As one who has a mother, father, and teacher should say' etc. (Bṛ. IV. i. 2). Or (*tribhiḥ* may mean) through the Vedas, the Smṛtis, and the good people; or through direct perception, inference, and the scriptures; for it is a matter of experience that clarity[1] follows from them. *Triṇāciketaḥ*, one who has piled up the Nāciketa fire thrice; or one who is possessed of its knowledge, studies it, and performs it; and *trikarmakṛt*, one who undertakes three kinds of *karma*—sacrifice, study (of the Vedas), and charity; *tarati*, crosses over; *janmamṛtyū*, birth and death. Moreover, *viditvā*, knowing—from scriptures; *brahmajajñam*: one that is born from Brahmā, i.e. Hiraṇyagarbha, is *brahmaja* (Virāṭ); and one who is *brahmaja* and *jña*, illumined, is *brahmajajña*—for He (i.e. Virāṭ) is omniscient; (knowing) that *devam*, Deity, who is so called because of His effulgence (which is the derivative meaning), i.e. One who is possessed of such attributes as knowledge; and who is *īḍyam*, praiseworthy (adorable); (and) *nicāyya*,

[1] 'Comprehension of duties etc.'—A.G.

looking (meditating) on (that Virāṭ)—as one's own Self;[1] (one) *atyantam*, fully; *eti*, gets; *imām*, this (palpable), that is patent to one's understanding; *śāntim*, peace, withdrawal (from objects). The idea is that through a combination of meditation and rites he attains the state of Virāṭ.[2]

Now he concludes the results of the knowledge about the Fire and of its piling up, as also the topic under discussion:

त्रिणाचिकेतस्त्रयमेतद्विदित्वा
य एवं विद्वाꣳश्चिनुते नाचिकेतम् ।
स मृत्युपाशान् पुरतः प्रणोद्य
शोकातिगो मोदते स्वर्गलोके ॥१८॥

18. 'One who performs the Nāciketa sacrifice thrice after having known these three (factors), and he who having known thus, accomplishes the Nāciketa sacrifice, casts off the snares of Death even

[1] ' "The number of bricks (in this sacrifice) is 720; the days and nights in a year (identified with Virāṭ Prajāpati) have also the same number. Because of this similarity of number the Fire (Year-Prajāpati) constituted by those days and nights, am I"—meditating on the Fire (Virāṭ) in this way as identified with oneself.'—A. G.

[2] Bālagopālendra's interpretation: 'Just as one who undertakes three kinds of work after getting connected with the three crosses over death, so does he who perform the Nāciketa sacrifice three times. Moreover, getting knowledge of that omniscient One who is born of Brahmā and realizing that One (as his Self), he attains this peace fully.'

earlier, and crossing over sorrow rejoices in heaven.

Viditvā, after knowing; *etat trayam*, these three—described earlier, 'the class and number of bricks, as also the manner of arranging for the fire' (I. i. 15); he who becomes *triṇāciketaḥ*, a performer of the Nāciketa sacrifice thrice; and *yaḥ*, who; *evam vidvān*, having known the Fire (Virāṭ) thus—as identified with oneself; *cinute*, accomplishes; *nāciketam*, the Nāciketa fire—performs the sacrifice called Nāciketa[1]; *saḥ*, he; *praṇodya*, casting off; *mṛtyupāśān*, the snares of Death—consisting in vice, ignorance, desire, hatred, etc.; *purataḥ*, even earlier—i. e. before death; *śokātigaḥ*, crossing over sorrow, i.e. freed from mental sorrow; *modate*, rejoices; *svargaloke*, in heaven, in the world of Virāṭ, by becoming identified with Him.

एष तेऽग्निर्नचिकेतः स्वर्ग्यो
यमवृणीथा द्वितीयेन वरेण।
एतमग्निं तवैव प्रवक्ष्यन्ति जनास-
स्तृतीयं वरं नचिकेतो वृणीष्व ॥१९॥

19. 'O Naciketā, this is for you the boon about the Fire that leads to heaven, for which you prayed through the second boon. People will speak of this Fire as yours indeed. O Naciketā, ask for the third boon.'

[1] 'Undertakes meditation on the Nāciketa Fire (i. e. Virāṭ)' according to Bālagopālendra, the word *kratu* in the commentary being taken in the sense of 'meditation'.

Naciketaḥ, O Naciketā; *te*, to you; *eṣaḥ*, this is; *svargyaḥ agniḥ*, the Fire—the boon about the Fire—that leads to heaven; *yam*, which—which Fire as a boon; *avṛṇīthāḥ*, you prayed for; *dvitīyena vareṇa*, through the second boon. That boon about the Fire is granted to you. This is only a conclusion of what was said earlier. Moreover, *janāsaḥ* (is the same as *janāḥ*), people; *pravakṣyanti*, will speak of; *etam agnim*, this Fire; *tava eva*, as yours—by your name—indeed. This is the fourth boon that I have given out of my satisfaction. *Naciketaḥ*, O Naciketā; *vṛṇīṣva*, ask for; *tṛtīyam varam*, the third boon. The idea is this: 'Unless that is given, I shall remain indebted.'

This much only, as indicated by the two boons, and not the true knowledge of the reality, called the Self, is attainable through the earlier *mantras* and *brāhmaṇas* (of the Vedas) which are concerned with injunction and prohibition. Hence, for the elimination of the natural ignorance, which is the seed of mundane existence, which consists in superimposing activity, agentship, and enjoyment on the Self, and which has for its contents those objects of prohibition and injunction (the subject matter of the scriptures), it is necessary to speak of the knowledge of the unity of the Self and Brahman—which knowledge is opposed to this ignorance, is devoid of any tinge of superimposition (on the Self) of activity, agentship, and enjoyment, and has for its object absolute emancipation. Therefore the subsequent text is begun. Through the story is being elaborated the fact as to how in the absence of the knowledge of the Self, which is the subject matter of the third boon, there cannot be any contentment even after getting the second boon. Since one who has desisted from the impermanent ends and means that are comprised in the abovementioned rites becomes qualified for the knowledge of the Self, therefore, with a view to decrying those ends and means, Naciketā is being tempted through the presentation of sons etc. Having been told, 'O Naciketā, you ask for the third boon', Naciketā said:

येयं प्रेते विचिकित्सा मनुष्ये-
ऽस्तीत्येके नायमस्तीति चैके ।
एतद्विद्यामनुशिष्टस्त्वयाऽहं
वराणामेष वरस्तृतीयः ॥२०॥

20. This doubt that arises, consequent on the death of a man—some saying, 'It exists', and others saying 'It does not exist'—I would know this, under your instruction. Of all the boons, this one is the third boon.

Yā iyam vicikitsā, this doubt, that arises; *prete manuṣye*, when a man dies; *eke*, some (say); *asti iti*, (It), the Self, which is distinct from the body, senses, mind, and intellect, and which gets connected with a fresh body (in the next life), exists; *ca eke*, and others (say); *ayam*, this one, a Self of this kind; *na asti*, does not exist. Hence It is a thing whose knowledge can be acquired by us neither through direct perception nor through inference. And yet the supreme human goal is dependent on a clear knowledge of It. Therefore, *tvayā anuśiṣṭaḥ*, being instructed by you; *aham*, I; *etat vidyām*, would know this. *Varāṇām*, of all the boons; *eṣaḥ*, this one; *varaḥ*, boon; is *tṛtīyaḥ*, the third—the remaining one.

With a view to testing whether this one (i.e. Naciketā) is absolutely fit or not for the knowledge of the Self, which (knowledge) is the means for the highest consummation, Death says:

देवैरत्रापि विचिकित्सितं पुरा
न हि सुविज्ञेयमणुरेष धर्मः।
अन्यं वरं नचिकेतो वृणीष्व
मा मोपरोत्सीरति मा सृजैनम् ॥२१॥

21. With regard to this, even the gods entertained doubts in days of yore; for being subtle, this substance (the Self) is not truly comprehended. O Naciketā, ask for some other boon; do not press me; give up this (boon) that is demanded of me.

Purā, in days of yore; *atra*, with regard to this thing; *vicikitsitam*, doubt was entertained; *devaiḥ api*, even by gods; *hi*, since; *eṣaḥ dharmaḥ*, this principle—called the Self; *na suvijñeyam*, is not truly[1] comprehensible—to common people, even though heard by them; It being *aṇuḥ*, subtle. Hence *naciketaḥ*, O Naciketā; *vṛṇīṣva*, you ask for; *anyam varam*, some other boon—whose result is not subject to doubt. *Mā up-*

[1] *Suvijñeyam* is also translated as 'easily comprehensible'.

arotsīḥ, do not press; *mā*, me—as a creditor does a debtor—*mā*, being the same as *mām* (me); *atisṛja*, give up; *enam*, this boon; that is directed towards *mā*, me (that is to say, demanded of me).

Being spoken to thus, Naciketā said:

देवैरत्रापि विचिकित्सितं किल
त्वं च मृत्यो यन्न सुज्ञेयमात्थ ।
वक्ता चास्य त्वादृगन्यो न लभ्यो
नान्यो वरस्तुल्य एतस्य कश्चित् ॥२२॥

22. Even the gods entertained doubt with regard to this thing; and O Death, since you too say that It is not truly comprehended and since any other instructor like you, of this thing, is not to be had, (therefore) there is no other boon comparable to this one.

'*Atra*, with regard to this thing; doubt was entertained even by the gods'—this has been heard by us from yourself. *Ca*, and; *mṛtyo*, O Death; *yat*, since; *tvam*, you; *āttha*, say; that the reality of the Self, *na sujñeyam*, is not truly comprehended; therefore, this thing being unknowable even to the learned; *vaktā ca asya*, an instructor of this principle; *anyaḥ*, anyone else—who is a learned man; *tvādṛk*, like you; *na labhyaḥ*, is not to be had—even by searching. But this boon is the means for the attainment of the highest goal. Hence *na anyaḥ varaḥ*, there is no other boon; *kaḥ cit*, whatsoever; which is *etasya tulyaḥ*, comparable to this one—since all the other bear impermanent fruits; this is the purport.

Although told thus, still Death says by way of tempting:

शतायुषः पुत्रपौत्रान्वृणीष्व
बहून्पशून् हस्तिहिरण्यमश्वान् ।
भूमेर्महदायतनं वृणीष्व
स्वयं च जीव शरदो यावदिच्छसि ॥२३॥

23. Ask for sons and grandsons that will be centenarians. Ask for many animals, elephants, and gold, and horses, and a vast expanse of the earth. And you yourself live for as many years as you like.

Vṛṇīṣva, you ask for; *putra-pautrān*, sons and grandsons; who are *śatāyuṣaḥ*, gifted with a hundred years of life. Moreover, *bahūn*, many; *paśūn*, animals, such as cows etc.; *hasti-hiraṇyam*, elephants and gold; and *aśvān*, horses. Besides, *vṛṇīṣva*, ask for; *mahat āyatanam*, a vast expanse, habitat, region, a kingdom; *bhūmeḥ*, of the earth. Furthermore, all this is useless if one is short-lived. Therefore he says: *ca*, and; *svayam*, you yourself; *jīva*, live, hold to your body with all the senses unimpaired; for as many *śaradaḥ*, years; *yāvat icchasi*, as you wish—to live.

एतत्तुल्यं यदि मन्यसे वरं
वृणीष्व वित्तं चिरजीविकां च ।

महाभूमौ नचिकेतस्त्वमेधि
कामानां त्वा कामभाजं करोमि ॥२४॥

24. If you think some other boon to be equal to this, ask for that. Ask for wealth and long life. O Naciketā, you become (a ruler) over a vast region. I make you fit for the enjoyment of (all) delectable things.

Yadi, if; *manyase*, you think; some other *varam*, boon; *etat-tulyam*, equal to this—as it has been presented; even that boon, *vṛṇīṣva*, you ask for. Moreover, (you ask for) *vittam*, wealth—plenty of gold, jewels, etc.; *ca cirajīvikām*, and long life—i. e. you ask for a long life together with wealth. In brief, *tvam*, you, Naciketā; *edhi*, become a king; *mahābhūmau*, over a vast region. Besides, *karomi*, I make; *tvā*, you; *kāmabhājam*, partaker of the enjoyment—fit for enjoyment; *kāmānām*, of enjoyable things—divine as well as human; for I am a deity whose will never fails.

ये ये कामा दुर्लभा मर्त्यलोके
सर्वान् कामाꣳश्छन्दतः प्रार्थयस्व ।
इमा रामाः सरथाः सतूर्या
न हीदृशा लम्भनीया मनुष्यैः ।
आभिर्मत्प्रत्ताभिः परिचारयस्व
नचिकेतो मरणं माऽनुप्राक्षीः ॥२५॥

25. Whatever things there be that are desirable but difficult to get—pray for all those cherished

things according to your choice. Here are these women with chariots and musical instruments—such are surely not to be had by mortals. With these, who are offered by me, you get yourself served. O Naciketā, do not inquire about death.

Ye ye, all things; that are *kāmāḥ*, desirable; and *durlabhāḥ*, difficult to get; *martyaloke*, in the human world; *sarvān kāmān*, all those desirable things; *prārthayasva*, ask for; *chandataḥ*, according to your choice. Moreover, *imāḥ*, here are; the celestial nymphs—the *rāmāḥ* (lit. women) who are so called because they delight (*ramayanti*) men; (and who are there) *sarathāḥ*, with chariots; and *satūryāḥ*, with musical instruments. *Īdṛśāḥ*, such (women); *na hi lambhanīyāḥ*, are surely not to be had—without the favour of persons like us; *manuṣyaiḥ*, by mortals. *Ābhiḥ*, by these—by these female attendants; *mat-prattābhiḥ*, who are offered by me; *paricārayasva*, get yourself served—i.e. get your own service performed, such as washing of feet etc. O Naciketā, *maraṇam*, of death—as to the problem of death, as to whether anything exists after the fall of the body or not, which question is (useless) like the examination of the teeth of a crow; *mā anuprākṣīḥ*, do not inquire—it does not befit you to ask thus.

Although tempted thus, Naciketā who, like a vast lake, was not to be perturbed, said:

श्वोभावा मर्त्यस्य यदन्तकैतत्
सर्वेन्द्रियाणां जरयन्ति तेजः ।

अपि सर्वं जीवितमल्पमेव
तवैव वाहास्तव नृत्यगीते ॥२६॥

26. O Death, ephemeral are these, and they waste away the vigour of all the organs that a man has. All life, without exception, is short indeed. Let the vehicles be yours alone; let the dances and songs be yours.

Antaka, O Death; the enjoyable things enumerated by you are *śvobhāvāḥ*, ephemeral—whose existence (*bhāvaḥ*) invariably is subject to the doubt as to whether they will exist or not tomorrow (*śvaḥ*); moreover, all those enjoyable things such as nymphs etc. *jarayanti*, waste away; *tejaḥ*, the vigour; *yat*, that (that there is); *sarvendriyāṇām*, of all the organs; *martyasya*, of a human being; so these enjoyable things are an evil since they wear away virtue, strength, intelligence, energy, fame, etc. As for long life which you wish to offer, about that too listen: *Sarvam api jīvitam*, all life—even that of Brahmā; is *alpam eva*, short indeed; what need be said of the longevity of those like us? Therefore, let *vāhāḥ*, the vehicles etc; and so also *nṛtyagīte*, the dances and songs; remain *tava eva*, yours alone.

न वित्तेन तर्पणीयो मनुष्यो
लप्स्यामहे वित्तमद्राक्ष्म चेत्त्वा ।
जीविष्यामो यावदीशिष्यसि त्वं
वरस्तु मे वरणीयः स एव ॥२७॥

27. Man is not to be satisfied with wealth. Now that we have met you, we shall get wealth. We shall live as long as you will rule. But the boon that is worth praying for by me is that alone.

Besides, *manuṣyaḥ*, man; *na tarpaṇīyaḥ*, is not to be satisfied; *vittena*, with wealth — in abundance; for the acquisition of wealth is not seen in this world to satisfy anyone. Should there arise in us any hankering for wealth, *lapsyāmahe*, we shall acquire, i.e. we shall get; *vittam*, wealth; *cet adrākṣma*, now that we have seen; *tvā*, you — *tvā* being the same as *tvām*, you. Thus, too, we shall get longevity. *Jīviṣyāmaḥ*, we shall live; *yāvat*, as long as; *tvam*, you; *īśiṣyasi* (should rather be *īśiṣyase*), will rule — lord it over in the position of Death. How can a man, after having met you, become poor or short-lived? *Varaḥ tu me varaṇīyaḥ saḥ eva*, but the boon that is worth praying for by me is that alone — that which is the knowledge of the Self.

अजीर्यताममृतानामुपेत्य
जीर्यन्मर्त्यः क्वधःस्थः प्रजानन् ।
अभिध्यायन् वर्णरतिप्रमोदा-
नतिदीर्घे जीविते को रमेत ॥२८॥

28. Having reached the proximity of the undecaying immortals, what decaying mortal who dwells on this lower region, the earth, but knows of higher goals, will take delight in a long life while conscious of the worthlessness of music, disport, and the joy thereof?

Further, *upetya*, having approached the proximity; *ajīryatām*, of the undecaying, of those who do not undergo the loss of age; *amṛtānām*, of the immortals; (and) *prajānan*, knowing, perceiving—that some other better benefit can be derived from them; but himself being *jīryan martyaḥ*, subject to decrepitude and death; (and himself) *kvadhaḥsthaḥ*, living on the earth—the word being dervied thus: *ku* is the earth and it is *adhaḥ*, below, in relation to the sky and other regions; one who lives (*tiṣṭhati*) there is *kvadhaḥsthaḥ*. (Being so) how can he ask for such evanescent things as sons, wealth, gold, etc. which are fit to be prayed for by the non-discriminating people? Or there may be a different reading—*kva tadāsthaḥ*—in which case the words are to be construed thus: *tadāsthaḥ* is one who has *āsthā*, absorption in, resorts to with absorption (*teṣu*) in those, sons etc; *kva* (means) where. (So the phrase means)—where will one, who wishes to achieve a human goal higher than that, difficult though it is to secure, become *tadāsthaḥ*, occupied with them? The idea is that nobody who knows their worthlessness will hanker after them. For every person verily wants to go higher and higher up. Therefore, I am not to be seduced by the lure of sons, wealth, etc. Moreover, *kaḥ*, who, what sensible man; *abhidhyāyan*, while deliberating on—ascertaining the real nature of; *varṇaratipramodān*, music, disport, and delight—derivable from celestial nymphs etc.; as transitory, *rameta*, will delight; *atidīrghe jīvite*, in a long life?

यस्मिन्निदं विचिकित्सन्ति मृत्यो
यत्साम्पराये महति ब्रूहि नस्तत् ।
योऽयं वरो गूढमनुप्रविष्टो
नान्यं तस्मान्नचिकेता वृणीते ॥२९॥

इति काठकोपनिषदि प्रथमाध्याये प्रथमा वल्ली ॥

29. O Death, tell us of that thing about which people entertain doubt in the context of the next world and whose knowledge leads to a great result. Apart from this boon, which relates to the inscrutable thing, Naciketā does not pray for any other.

Hence give up alluring me with transitory things, and *brūhi naḥ*, tell us; *tat*, that, which is prayed for by me; *yasmin*, about which—which Self; people *idam vicikitsanti*, entertain this doubt—as to whether it exists or not; *sāmparāye*, in the context of the next world—when a man dies; *yat*, which—which conclusive knowledge of the Self; *mahati*, is calculated to lead to a great result. To be brief, *ayam varaḥ*, this boon—that relates to the Self under discussion; *yaḥ*, which (boon); *gūḍham anupraviṣṭaḥ*, has entered into an inaccessible recess—has become very inscrutable; apart from that boon *anyam*, any other—any boon with regard to the non-Self that can be sought after by senseless people; *naciketā na vṛṇīte*, Naciketā does not pray for—even in thought. This (last sentence) is a statement by the Upaniṣad itself (and is not an utterance of Naciketā).

PART I

Canto II

Having tested the disciple and found his fitness for knowledge, he (Yama) said:

अन्यच्छ्रेयोऽन्यदुतैव प्रेय-
स्ते उभे नानार्थे पुरुषꣳ सिनीतः ।
तयोः श्रेय आददानस्य साधु
भवति हीयतेऽर्थाद्य उ प्रेयो वृणीते ॥१॥

1. The preferable is different indeed; and so, indeed, is the pleasurable different. These two, serving divergent purposes, (as they do), bind men. Good befalls him who accepts the preferable among these two. He who selects the pleasurable, falls from the true end.

Śreyaḥ, the preferable, the supreme goal (freedom); *anyat eva*, (is) certainly different. Similarly, *uta*, too; *preyaḥ*, the more pleasant; *anyat eva*, (is) different indeed. *Te ubhe*, both of them — the pleasurable and the preferable; *nānā arthe*, serving divergent purposes — as they do; *sinītaḥ*, bind; *puruṣam*, man — one who, as subject to caste, stage of life, etc., is competent (for either). All men are impelled by these two under an idea of personal duty; for according as one hankers after prosperity or immortality, one engages in the pleasurable or the preferable. Therefore, all men are said to be bound by these two through their sense of duty with regard to what leads to the pleasurable or the preferable. These two, though related severally to the (two) human goals[1], are opposed to each other, inasmuch as they are of the nature of knowledge and ignorance. Thus since these cannot be performed together by the same person, without discarding either of the two, therefore *tayoḥ*, of the two; *ādadānasya*, to one who accepts; only *śreyaḥ*, the preferable, by discarding the pleasurable, (the latter) being of the nature of ignorance; *sādhu bhavati*, well-being, good, comes (as a result). But he who is a short-sighted, the ignorant man, *hīyate*, gets alienated; *arthāt*, from this objective, from the human goal, i.e. he falls from the eternal supreme purpose. Who is that man? *Yaḥ u*, the one that; *preyaḥ vṛṇīte*, selects, i.e. takes hold of, the pleasurable.

If both can be done by a man at will, why do people cling mostly to the pleasurable only? This is being answered:

श्रेयश्च प्रेयश्च मनुष्यमेत-
स्तौ सम्परीत्य विविनक्ति धीरः।
श्रेयो हि धीरोऽभि प्रेयसो वृणीते
प्रेयो मन्दो योगक्षेमाद्वृणीते ॥२॥

2. The preferable and the pleasurable approach man. The man of intelligence, having considered

[1] (i) Prosperity here and hereafter, and (ii) salvation.

them, separates the two. The intelligent one selects the electable in preference to the delectable; the non-intelligent one selects the delectable for the sake of growth and protection (of the body etc.).

True it is that they are subject to (human) option; still, since they are not easily distinguishable by men of poor intellect, either with regard to their means or with regard to their fruits, therefore, *śreyaśca preyaśca*, the preferable and the pleasurable; *manuṣyam etaḥ* (*ā-itaḥ*), approach this man, as though they are intermixed. Therefore, just as a swan separates milk from water, similarly *dhīraḥ*, a man of intelligence; *samparītya*, having surveyed fully, having considered mentally their importance and unimportance; *vivinakti*, separates; *tau*, those two, viz the preferable and the pleasurable things. And having distinguished, *śreyaḥ hi*, the electable indeed; *abhivṛṇīte*, (he) selects, because of its higher value; *preyasaḥ*, in comparison with the delectable. Who is he (that perfers)? *Dhīraḥ*, the intelligent man. As for the *mandaḥ*, the man of poor intelligence; he, because of a lack of discrimination, *yogakṣemāt*, for the sake of *yoga* and *kṣema*, i.e. for the growth and protection of the body etc.; *vṛṇīte*, selects; *preyaḥ*, the delectable, constituted by cattle, sons, etc.

स त्वं प्रियान्प्रियरूपांश्च कामा-
नभिध्यायन्नचिकेतोऽत्यस्राक्षीः ।
नैतां सृङ्कां वित्तमयीमवाप्तो
यस्यां मज्जन्ति बहवो मनुष्याः ॥३॥

3. O Naciketā! you, such as you are, have discarded, after consideration, all the desirable things that are themselves delightful or are the producers of delight. You have not accepted this path of wealth in which many a man comes to grief.

Saḥ tvam, you, such as you are—though tempted by me again and again; *abhidhyāyan*, having considered—the defects such as impermanence and insubstantiality of; *kāmān*, desirable things; viz *priyān*, dear ones, such as children etc.; *ca*, and; *priyarūpān*, producers of delight, such as nymphs etc.[1]; *naciketaḥ*, O Naciketā; *atyasrākṣīḥ*, you have discarded. What an intelligence you have! *Na avāptaḥ*, you have not accepted; *etām*, this; ugly *sṛṅkām*, course; *vittamayīm*, abounding in wealth, which is resorted to by ignorant people; *yasyām*, in which course; *bahavaḥ*, many; *manuṣyāḥ*, men; *majjanti*, sink, come to grief.

It has been said, 'Good befalls him who accepts the preferable among these two. He who selects the pleasurable, falls from the true end.' (I.ii.1) Why is that so? Because:

दूरमेते विपरीते विषूची
अविद्या या च विद्येति ज्ञाता ।
विद्याभीप्सिनं नचिकेतसं मन्ये
न त्वा कामा बहवोऽलोलुपन्त ॥४॥

[1] Children are one's own Self, as it were, whereas nymphs are a degree removed from one.

4. That which is known as knowledge and that which is known as ignorance are widely contradictory, and they follow divergent courses. I consider Naciketā to be an aspirant for knowledge, (because) the enjoyable things, multifarious though they be, did not tempt you.

Ete, these two; are *dūram*, widely, by a great distance; *viparīte*, contradictory, mutually exclusive, like light and darkness, they being of the nature of discrimination and non-discrimination; *viṣūcī* (i.e. *viṣūcyau*), have divergent courses, i.e. they produce different results, being the causes of worldly existence and emancipation. This is the idea. Which are they? The answer is: *Yā ca*, that which; *jñātā*, is fully ascertained, known by the learned; *avidyā iti*, as ignorance—which has for its object the pleasurable; *yā ca*, and that which; (is known) *vidyā iti*, as knowledge—which has for its object the preferable. Of these two, *manye*, I consider; you *naciketasam*, Naciketā; *vidyābhīpsinam*, as desirous of knowledge. Why? Because, *kāmāḥ*, the enjoyable things, such as nymphs etc.—which distract the intellect of the unenlightened; although they are *bahavaḥ*, many; they *na alolupanta*, did not tempt; *tvā*, you—*tvā* being the same as *tvām*; did not deflect you from the path of the preferable by arousing a desire for enjoying them. Therefore, I consider you to be craving for enlightenment, to be fit for the preferable—this is the idea.

अविद्यायामन्तरे वर्तमानाः
स्वयं धीराः पण्डितंमन्यमानाः ।

दन्द्रम्यमाणाः परियन्ति मूढा
अन्धेनैव नीयमाना यथान्धाः ॥५॥

5. Living in the midst of ignorance and considering themselves intelligent and enlightened, the senseless people go round and round, following crooked courses, just like the blind led by the blind.

But those who are fit for worldly existence, they, *vartamānāḥ*, living; *avidyāyām antare*, in the midst of ignorance—as though in the midst of thick darkness, being entangled in hundreds of fetters, forged by craving for sons, cattle, etc.; *manyamānāḥ*, considering—thinking of themselves; '*svayam*, we ourselves are; *dhīrāḥ*, intelligent; and *paṇḍitāḥ*, versed in the scriptures'; those *mūḍhāḥ*, senseless, non-discriminating people; *pariyanti*, go round and round; *dandramyamāṇāḥ*, by following[1] very much the various crooked courses, being afflicted by old age, death, disease, etc.; just as many *andhāḥ*, blind people; *nīyamānāḥ*, being led; *andhena eva*, by the blind indeed, on an uneven road, come to great calamity.

Because of this alone, because of ignorance, the means for the attainment of the other world does not become revealed (to them):

न साम्परायः प्रतिभाति बालं
प्रमाद्यन्तं वित्तमोहेन मूढम् ।

[1] Our reading is *gacchantaḥ*. A different reading is *icchantaḥ*, wishing for.

अयं लोको नास्ति पर इति मानी
पुनः पुनर्वशमापद्यते मे ॥६॥

6. The means for the attainment of the other world does not become revealed to the non-discriminating man who blunders, being befooled by the lure of wealth. One that constantly thinks that there is only this world, and none hereafter, comes under my sway again and again.

Samparāyaḥ is the other world, attainable after the falling of the body (*sampara*); *Sāmparāyaḥ* is any particular scriptural means leading to the attainment of that other world. And this (means) *na pratibhāti*, does not become revealed, i.e. does not become serviceable; *bālam*, to a boy, to a non-discriminating man; (who is) *pramādyantam*, blundering —whose mind clings to such needs as children, cattle, etc.; and so also who is *mūḍham*, confounded, being covered by darkness (of ignorance); *vittamohena*, because of the non-discrimination caused by wealth. '*Ayam lokaḥ*, there is only this world—that which is visible and abounds with women, food, drink, etc.; *na paraḥ asti*, there is no other world, that is invisible' —*iti mānī*, constantly thinking thus; (he) getting born, *punaḥ punaḥ*, again and again; *āpadyate*, becomes subject to; the *vaśam*, control; *me*, of me, who am Death; that is, he remains involved in a succession of grief in the form of birth, death, etc. Such is the world in general.

But among thousands, it is only one like you who

hankers after the preferable, and who becomes a knower of the Self. Because:

श्रवणायापि बहुभिर्यो न लभ्यः
शृण्वन्तोऽपि बहवो यं न विद्युः ।
आश्चर्यो वक्ता कुशलोऽस्य लब्धाऽऽ-
श्चर्यो ज्ञाता कुशलानुशिष्टः ॥७॥

7. Of that (Self), which is not available for the mere hearing to many, (and) which many do not understand even while hearing, the expounder is wonderful and the receiver is wonderful; wonderful is he who knows under the instruction of an adept.

Yaḥ, that which—the Self that; *na labhyaḥ*, is not attainable; *bahubhiḥ*, by many; *śravaṇāya api*, even for the sake of hearing; *yam*, which—which Self; *bahavaḥ*, many (others); *śṛṇvantaḥ api*, even while hearing; *na vidyuḥ* (*vidanti*), do not know; the unfortunate whose minds have not been purified may not know. Moreover, even *asya vaktā*, Its expounder; (is) *āścaryaḥ*, wonderful—comparable to a wonder—a rare one, indeed, among many. Similarly, even after hearing of this Self, *kuśalaḥ*, one who is proficient—a rare one among many; becomes the *labdhā*, attainer. For *āścaryaḥ jñātā*, a wonderful man—a rare soul—becomes a knower; *kuśalānuśiṣṭaḥ*, being instructed by a proficient teacher.

Why (so)? Because:

न नरेणावरेण प्रोक्त एष
सुविज्ञेयो बहुधा चिन्त्यमानः ।
अनन्यप्रोक्ते गतिरत्र नास्ति
अणीयान् ह्यतर्क्यमणुप्रमाणात् ॥८॥

8. The Self is not certainly adequately known when spoken of by an inferior person; for It is thought of variously. When taught by one who has become identified with It, there is no further cogitation with regard to It. For It is beyond argumentation, being subtler even than the atomic quantity.

Eṣaḥ, this—the Self about whom you ask me; (when) *proktaḥ*, spoken of; *avareṇa nareṇa*, by an inferior man, i. e. by a man of worldly understanding; *na hi suvijñeyaḥ*, is not certainly capable of being adequately understood; for It is *bahudhā*, variously—such as 'It exists', 'It does not exist', 'It is the doer', 'It is not the doer', 'It is pure', 'It is impure', etc.; *cintyamānaḥ*, deliberated on—by disputants. How, again, is It well understood? This is being said: The Self *ananyaprokte*, when spoken of by a non-different man, by the teacher who does not see duality, who has become identified with the Brahman that is to be revealed (by him[1]); *atra*, here, with regard to the Self; *na asti*, there does not remain; *gatiḥ*, cogitation, of various kinds as to whether It exists or not; for from the Self is ruled out all thoughts involving doubt.

[1] Or, 'revealed in the Upaniṣads'—Bālagopālendra.

Or—*ananyaprokte*, when the (supreme) Self, that is non-different from, and is, one's very Self, is adequately taught[1]; *na asti gatiḥ*, there is no other comprehension[2]; *atra*, of this Self; because there is nothing else[3] to be known. For the realization of the unity of the Self is the culmination of all knowledge. Therefore, as there is no knowable, there remains nothing to be known here.

Or—when the non-different Self is spoken of, *na asti atra gatiḥ*, there remains no transmigration[4]; for emancipation, which is the result of that realization, follows immediately.

Or—when the Self is spoken of by a teacher who has become identified with Brahman that he speaks of, there is *na agatiḥ*, no non-comprehension, non-realization. To this hearer the realization about that Self does come as, 'I am that (Self)', just as it did in the case of the teacher. This is the idea.

Thus is the Self well understood when It is taught to be non-different (from the taught) by a teacher who is well versed in the scriptures.[5] Else the Self

[1] Or, 'taught as non-different from, and as, one's very Self'—Bālagopālendra.

[2] Apart from the realization: 'I am Brahman.'

[3] Apart from the unity of the Self and Brahman.

[4] Bālagopālendra interprets *saṁsāra-gati* as the appearance of duality as a reality. This appearance ceases after Self-knowledge.

[5] 'When It is taught by a teacher, well versed in the scriptures and established in a state of non-difference'—Bālagopālendra.

becomes *aṇīyān*, more subtle; even *aṇupramāṇāt*, than an atomic thing. (For It is) *atarkyam* (should be *atarkyaḥ*), cannot be argued out—cannot be known through mere reasoning called up through one's own (independent) intellect[1]. For if the Self be regarded as an object of argumentation and postulated to be atomic in quantity, someone else may hold It to be subtler than that, while still another may hold It to be the subtlest. Thus there is no finality about sophistry.

नैषा तर्केण मतिरापनेया
प्रोक्तान्येनैव सुज्ञानाय प्रेष्ठ ।
यां त्वमापः सत्यधृतिर्बतासि
त्वादृङ्नो भूयान्नचिकेतः प्रष्टा ॥९॥

9. This wisdom that you have, O dearest one, which leads to sound knowledge when imparted only by someone else (other than the logician), is not to be attained through argumentation. You are, O compassionable one, endowed with true resolution. May our questioner be like you, O Naciketā.

Therefore *eṣā*, this—this wisdom about the Self, as presented by Vedas, that arises when the Self is taught by one who has become identified with It; *na āpaneyā*, i.e. *na prāpaṇīyā*, is not to be attained; *tarkeṇa*, through argumentation—called up merely

[1] As distinguished from the intellect purified by the teaching of an adept.

by one's own intellect. Or (reading the word as *ā-apaneyā*, the expression *na āpaneyā* means), should not be eradicated, should not be destroyed. For, a logician who is not versed in the Vedas, talks of all sorts of things that can be called up by his own intellect. Therefore, *preṣṭha*, O dearest one; this wisdom that originates from the Vedas, *sujñānāya* (*bhavati*), leads to sound knowledge; when *proktā*, imparted; *anyena eva*, by a different person indeed—by a teacher who is versed in the Vedas and is different from the logician. What, again, is that belief which is beyond argumentation? This is being said: *yām*, that which—the wisdom that; *tvam āpah*, you have attained, through the granting of the boon by me. *Asi*, you are; *satyadhṛtiḥ*, of true resolution—your resolves refer to real things. Death utters the word *bata* (a particle expressing compassion) out of compassion for Naciketā, thereby eulogizing the knowledge that is going to be imparted. Any other *praṣṭā*, questioner—whether a son or a disciple; (that there may be) *naḥ*, to us; *bhūyāt*, may he be; *tvādṛk*, like you. Of what sort? The kind of questioner that you are; *naciketaḥ*, O Naciketā.

Being pleased, he said again:

जानाम्यहं शेवधिरित्यनित्यं
न ह्यध्रुवैः प्राप्यते हि ध्रुवं तत्।
ततो मया नाचिकेतश्चितोऽग्नि-
रनित्यैर्द्रव्यैः प्राप्तवानस्मि नित्यम् ॥१०॥

10. (Since) I know that this treasure is imper-

manent—for that permanent entity cannot be attained through impermanent things—therefore, (knowingly) did I pile up the Nāciketa fire with impermanent things, and have (thereby) attained (relative) permanence.

Aham jānāmi, I know; *iti*, (this fact) that; *śevadhiḥ*, the treasure—comprising the fruits of action, which are prayed for like a treasure; that (treasure) is *anityam* (rather *anityaḥ*), impermanent. *Hi*, for; *adhruvaiḥ*, through impermanent things; *tat*, that; *dhruvam*, permanent entity—which is the treasure called the supreme Self; *na prāpyate*, cannot be attained. But that treasure alone, which consists of impermanent pleasure, is attained through impermanent things. *Hi*, since, this is so; *tataḥ*, therefore; *mayā*, by me—knowing as I did, that the permanent cannot be attained through evanescent means; *nāciketaḥ agniḥ*, the fire called Nāciketa; *citaḥ*, was piled up, i.e. the sacrifice that is meant for the acquisition of heavenly bliss, was accomplished; *anityaiḥ dravyaiḥ*, with impermanent things—by animals etc. Having acquired the requisite merit thereby, *prāptavān asmi*, I have achieved; *nityam*, the permanent—the relatively permanent abode of Death, which is called heaven.

कामस्याप्तिं जगतः प्रतिष्ठां
क्रतोरनन्त्यमभयस्य पारम् ।
स्तोममहदुरुगायं प्रतिष्ठां दृष्ट्वा
धृत्या धीरो नचिकेतोऽत्यस्राक्षीः ॥११॥

11. O Naciketā, you, on becoming enlightened, have rejected (them all) by examining patiently the highest reach of desire, the support of the universe, the infinite[1] results of meditation, the other shore of fearlessness, the extensive course (of Hiraṇyagarbha) that is praiseworthy and great, as also (your own) state.

But you, *dṛṣṭvā*, having seen (examined); (Hiraṇyagarbha as) *kāmasya āptim*, the end of desire—that here indeed all desires end[2] (vide Mu. III. ii. 2); having seen (Hiraṇyagarbha as) *jagataḥ pratiṣṭhām*, the support—because of His all-pervasiveness—of the world comprising all that is personal, elemental, heavenly, etc.; (having seen) the *anantyam*, i.e. *ānantyam*, infinitude; *kratoḥ*, of meditation[3]—the (relatively infinite) result (of meditation on Hiraṇyagarbha), which is the state of Hiraṇyagarbha; (having seen) *pāram*, the other shore, the utmost limit; *abhayasya*, of fearlessness; (having seen) the *urugāyam*, course (of Hiraṇyagarbha) that is extensive[4]; (and) which is *stoma-mahat*: that which is *stoma*, praiseworthy, and *mahat*, great—abounding in many attributes such as divine faculties of becoming subtle etc.—is *stoma-mahat*, because it is possessed

[1] All these are to be understood in a relative sense.

[2] Here, i.e. in the state of Hiraṇyagarbha. Desire cannot lead men beyond Hiraṇyagarbha.

[3] This is according to Bālagopālendra. Some translate it as 'of sacrifice'.

[4] Since thereby is attained the state of Hiraṇyagarbha which lasts for a long time till final dissolution.

of super-excellence; (and having seen) *pratiṣṭhām*, existence—your own state, unsurpassable though it is; *naciketaḥ*, O Naciketā; (having seen all these) *dhṛtyā*, with patience; and having become, *dhīraḥ*, intelligent; *atyasrākṣīḥ*, you have renounced—have given up all these worldly enjoyments (up to the state of Hiraṇyagarbha), being desirous only of the supreme One. O! what an unsurpassable quality you are endowed with!

तं दुर्दर्शं गूढमनुप्रविष्टं
गुहाहितं गह्वरेष्ठं पुराणम् ।
अध्यात्मयोगाधिगमेन देवं
मत्वा धीरो हर्षशोकौ जहाति ॥१२॥

12. The intelligent man gives up happiness and sorrow by developing concentration of mind on the Self and thereby meditating on the old Deity who is inscrutable, lodged inaccessibly, located in the intellect, and seated in the midst of misery.

Tam, Him—the Self that you want to know; which is *durdarśam*, hard to see, because of Its extreme subtleness; *gūḍham anupraviṣṭam*, lodged inaccessibly, i.e. hidden by knowledge that changes in accordance with worldly objects; *guhāhitam*, located in the intellect—because It is perceived there; *gahvareṣṭham*, existing in the midst of misery—in the body and senses which are the sources of many miseries. Since It is thus lodged inaccessibly and located in the intellect, therefore, It is seated in the midst of misery.

Hence It is hard to see. *Matvā*, meditating on; that *purāṇam*, old (everlasting); *devam*, Deity—the Self; *adhyātmayogādhigamena*—concentration of the mind on the Self after withdrawing it from the outer objects is *adhyātma-yoga*—through the attainment of that; *dhīraḥ*, the intelligent man; *jahāti*, gives up; *harṣaśokau*, happiness and sorrow—since there is no excellence or deterioration for the Self.

एतच्छ्रुत्वा सम्परिगृह्य मर्त्यः
प्रवृह्य धर्म्यमणुमेतमाप्य ।
स मोदते मोदनीयꣳ हि लब्ध्वा
विवृतꣳ सद्म नचिकेतसं मन्ये ॥१३॥

13. After hearing this, grasping it fully, separating this righteous thing (from the body etc.), and attaining this subtle thing, that mortal rejoices, for he has obtained that which is the cause of delight. I consider that the mansion (of Brahman) is wide open to Naciketā.

Moreover, a mortal who is subject to death, *śrutvā*, after hearing—through the favour of the teacher; *etat*, this reality of the Self that I shall speak of; *samparigṛhya*, after grasping (It) fully—as one's own Self; *pravṛhya*, after separating (from body etc.); this *dharmyam*, righteous[1] (thing, the Self); and *āpya*, after attaining; *etam aṇum*, this subtle thing—

[1] Lit. that which is conducive to virtue, the knowledge of Reality being the highest virtue.

the Self; *saḥ martyaḥ*, that mortal—(who has become) the enlightened man; *modate*, rejoices; *labdhvā*, having obtained; *modanīyam*, that which causes delight. Therefore, *manye*, I consider; that this *sadma*, mansion—the abode of Brahman, which is of this kind; *vivṛtam*, is wide open to—has approached towards[1]; *naciketasam*, (you) Naciketā. The idea is: 'I consider you fit for emancipation.'

(Naciketā said): 'If I am fit and you, too, sir, are pleased with me, then

अन्यत्र धर्मादन्यत्राधर्मा-
दन्यत्रास्मात्कृताकृतात् ।
अन्यत्र भूताच्च भव्याच्च
यत्तत्पश्यसि तद्वद ॥१४॥

14. 'Tell (me) of that thing which you see as different from virtue, different from vice, different from this cause and effect, and different from the past and the future.'

Anyatra dharmāt, different from virtue—i.e. from the performance of scriptural duties, their results, and their accessories; so also *anyatra adharmāt*, different from vice; so also *anyatra asmāt kṛtākṛtāt*, different from this *kṛta*, the effect, and *akṛta*, the cause; moreover, *anyatra bhūtāt ca bhavyāt ca*, dif-

[1] Brahman and the mansion are identical, and the approach of this mansion towards Naciketā consists in the propitiousness of Brahman.

ferent from the past time, and from the future—as also the present—i. e. what is not limited by the three times (past, present, and future); *yat*, what—the thing of this kind that is beyond the reach of all empirical experience, which; *paśyasi*, you see, you know; *tat*, that thing; *vada*, you tell—me.

With a view to speaking of the thing asked for, as also some other attributes, Death said to him who had inquired, thus:

सर्वे वेदा यत्पदमामनन्ति
तपाꣳसि सर्वाणि च यद्वदन्ति।
यदिच्छन्तो ब्रह्मचर्यं चरन्ति
तत्ते पदꣳ संग्रहेण ब्रवीम्योमित्येतत् ॥१५॥

15. I tell you briefly of that goal which all the Vedas with one voice propound, which all the austerities speak of, and wishing for which people practise Brahmacarya: it is this, viz *Om*.

Yat padam, that attainable thing—the goal, which; *sarve vedāḥ*, all the Vedas—without divergence; *āmananti*, propound; *ca*, and; *yat*, that which; *sarvāṇi tapāṁsi*, all the austerities; *vadanti*, speak of—i. e. are meant for the attainment of; *yat icchantaḥ*, wishing for which; *caranti*, (they) practise; *brahmacaryam*, Brahmacarya that either consists in residence (for study) in the house of the teacher or is of some other kind (i.e. lifelong celibacy) meant for the attainment of Brahman; *bravīmi*, I tell; *te*, you; *saṁgraheṇa*, in brief; *tat*, that; *padam*, goal, which you want to know: *Om iti etat*, it is this, viz *Om*. The goal that you desire to know is this that is indicated by the word *Om* and that has *Om* as its symbol.[1]

(Since *Om* is the name and symbol of Brahman), therefore:

एतद्ध्येवाक्षरं ब्रह्म एतद्ध्येवाक्षरं परम् ।
एतद्ध्येवाक्षरं ज्ञात्वा यो यदिच्छति तस्य तत् ॥१६॥

16. This letter (*Om*), indeed, is the (inferior) Brahman (Hiranyagarbha); and this letter is, indeed, the supreme Brahman. Anybody, who, (while) meditating on this letter, wants any of the two, to him comes that.

Etat eva akṣaram brahma, this letter (*Om*), indeed, is (the inferior) Brahman (Hiraṇyagarbha). And *etat eva akṣaram param*, this letter (*Om*) is the supreme

[1] It is well known that the thing that is revealed (i.e. flashes in the mind) on the utterance of a word is signified by that word. Thus the knowledge, untouched by outer objects, that reveals itself to the man of concentrated mind on the utterance of the word *Om*, is also dependent on and signified by *Om*. One should meditate thus: 'I am Brahman, as signified by *Om* and as conditioned by Māyā in which the *sattva* quality preponderates.' If, however, one is not able to do so, one should superimpose the idea of Brahman on the symbol *Om*. The best minds can think of Brahman without *Om*. The middle ones can meditate on Brahman with the help of *Om*. And the inferior ones can worship Brahman in the symbol *Om*.

Brahman. For of them both, this letter (*Om*) is the symbol. *Jñātvā*, (while) worshipping; *etat eva akṣaram*, this very letter *Om* as Brahman; anything that—whether the supreme or the inferior Brahman; *yaḥ*, anybody; *icchati*, wishes for; *tat tasya*, that becomes his: if it is the supreme Brahman (that he desires), It becomes knowable; if it is the inferior Brahman, It becomes attainable.

एतदालम्बनꣳ श्रेष्ठमेतदालम्बनं परम्।
एतदालम्बनं ज्ञात्वा ब्रह्मलोके महीयते॥१७॥

17. This medium is the best; this medium is the supreme (and the inferior) Brahman. Meditating on this medium, one becomes adorable in the world of Brahman.

Since this is so, therefore, among all the mediums (e.g. *Gāyatrī*), for the attainment of Brahman, *etat ālambanam*, this medium; is *śreṣṭham*, the highest—the most praiseworthy; *etat ālambanam*, this medium; (is) *param*, the supreme Brahman—as well as the inferior Brahman, since it relates to both the inferior Brahman and the supreme Brahman. *Jñātvā*, meditating on; *etat ālambanam*, this medium; *brahmaloke mahīyate*, one is worshipped in the world of Brahman. The idea is this: Getting identified with the supreme Brahman or the inferior Brahman, (as a result of meditation), he becomes adorable like Brahman.

For those aspirants of medium and inferior quality, *Om* has been indicated both as a medium (for meditation on), and a symbol (for worship) of, the Self which is devoid of all attributes and which was inquired about in 'Tell me of that thing which you see as different from virtue', etc. (I.ii.14); and It has also been presented similarly, for similar aspirants, who wish to know the inferior Brahman.

Now this is being said with a view to ascertaining directly the nature of that Self which has *Om* as Its medium:

न जायते म्रियते वा विपश्चि-
न्नायं कुतश्चिन्न बभूव कश्चित् ।
अजो नित्यः शाश्वतोऽयं पुराणो
न हन्यते हन्यमाने शरीरे ॥१८॥

18. The intelligent Self is neither born nor does It die. It did not originate from anything, nor did anything originate from It. It is birthless, eternal, undecaying, and ancient. It is not injured even when the body is killed.

Vipaścit, the intelligent One (Self)—intelligent, because Its nature of consciousness is never lost; *na jāyate*, is not born—It is not produced; *na vā mriyate*, nor does It die. An impermanent thing that has origination, is subject to many modifications. With a view to denying all the modifications in the Self, the first and last of these modifications, in the form of birth and death, are being first denied here in the text: 'He is neither born nor dies.' Moreover, *ayam*, this One—the Self; *na kutaścit*, did not come from anything—did not originate from any other cause; and from the Self Itself *na kaścit babhūva*, nothing originated—as something different from It. Therefore, *ayam*, this Self; (is) *ajaḥ*, birthless; *nityaḥ*, eternal; *śāśvataḥ*, undecaying. That which is impermanent is subject to decay, but this one is everlasting; therefore, again, It is *purāṇaḥ*, ancient—new indeed even in the past. A thing is said to be new now, which emerges into being through the development of its parts, as for instance, a pot etc. The Self, however, is opposed to them; It is ancient, i.e. devoid of growth. Since this is so, therefore, *na hanyate*, It is not killed—not injured; *śarīre hanyamāne*, when the body is killed—with weapons etc.—though It exists there, just like space.

हन्ता चेन्मन्यते हन्तुꣳ हतश्चेन्मन्यते हतम् ।
उभौ तौ न विजानीतो नायꣳ हन्ति न हन्यते ॥१९॥

19. If the killer thinks (of It) in terms of killing and if the killed thinks (of It) as killed, both of them do not know. It does not kill, nor is It killed.

Even though the Self is of this kind, still *cet*, if; someone who looks upon the mere body as the Self, *manyate*, thinks—of It; *hantum*, for the sake of killing—(if he) thinks, 'I shall kill It'; and the other who is *hatah*, killed; *cet*, if; he too, should *manyate*, think; the Self to be *hatam*, killed—(if he) thinks, 'I am killed'; *ubhau tau*, both of them, equally; *na vijānītaḥ*, do not know—their own Self; because *ayam*, this One; *na hanti*, does not kill—the Self being unchangeable; similarly, *na hanyate*, It is not killed—because of the very fact of unchangeability, as in the case of space. Therefore, the worldly existence, consisting of virtue and vice, relates merely to the ignorant man; it does not belong to the knower of Brahman, because for him virtue and vice are inappropriate according to both the Vedic authority and logic.

How, again, does one know the Self? This is being said:

अणोरणीयान्महतो महीया-
नात्माऽस्य जन्तोर्निहितो गुहायाम् ।
तमक्रतुः पश्यति वीतशोको
धातुप्रसादान्महिमानमात्मनः ॥२०॥

20. The Self that is subtler than the subtle and greater than the great, is lodged in the heart of (every) creature. A desireless man sees that glory of the Self through the serenity of the organs, and (thereby he becomes) free from sorrow.

(The Self is) *aṇīyān*, subtler; *aṇoḥ*, than the subtle—such as a (tiny) *śyāmāka* grain; *mahīyān*, greater; *mahataḥ*, than the great—things that have a great dimension, such as the earth. Whatever great or atomic thing there be in the world, can be so by being possessed of its reality through that eternal Self. When deprived of that Self, it is reduced to unreality. Therefore, that very Self is subtler than the subtle and greater than the great, for It is conditioned by all names, forms, and activities which are Its limiting adjuncts. And that *ātmā*, Self; *nihitaḥ*, is lodged, i.e. exists as the Self; *guhāyām*, in the heart; *asya jantoḥ*, of this creature—(in the heart) of all beings beginning from Brahmā and ending with a clump of grass. *Tam*, that Self—the means for whose realization are hearing, thinking, and meditation[1]; (he sees, who is) *akratuḥ*, a desireless man, i.e. one whose intellect has been withdrawn from all outer objects, seen or unseen; and when this (detachment) takes place, *dhātavaḥ*, the organs, such as mind etc. become composed, the *dhātus* being so called because of their holding (*dhāraṇa*) the body. (So) *dhātu-prasādāt*, through the serenity of these organs; (he) *paśyati*, sees; *tam mahimānam*, that glory; *ātmanaḥ*, of the Self—which is not subject to growth and decay in accordance with the result of work: he sees, i.e. he directly realizes the Self as 'I am the Self', and thereby he becomes *vītaśokaḥ*, free from sorrow.

Otherwise, the Self is difficult to be known by ordinary people who are possessed of desire, because:

आसीनो दूरं व्रजति शयानो याति सर्वतः ।
कस्तं मदामदं देवं मदन्यो ज्ञातुमर्हति ॥२१॥

21. While sitting, It travels far away; while sleep-

[1] This is according to Bālagopālendra. The phrase *darśana-śravaṇa-manana-vijñāna-liṅgam* may also mean, 'the Self whose existence is inferable from the acts of seeing, hearing, thinking, and knowing'.

ing, It goes everywhere. Who but I can know that Deity who is both joyful and joyless?

(The Self) while *āsīnaḥ*, sitting—remaining stationary, motionless; *dūram vrajati*, goes far; *śayānaḥ*, while sleeping; *yāti*, goes; *sarvataḥ*, everywhere. Similarly, that Deity, the Self, is *madāmadaḥ*, possessed of *mada*, and devoid of *mada*—joyful and joyless—possessed of contradictory qualities. Hence, it being difficult to know It, *kaḥ*, who; *madanyaḥ*, apart from me; *jñātum arhati*, can know; *tam madāmadam devam*, that joyful and joyless Deity? It is only by a wise man of fine intellect, like us, that this Self can be known well. Since the Self, as conditioned by various contradictory limiting adjuncts, is possessed of opposite qualities like rest and motion, permanence and impermanence, etc., therefore It appears variously like a prism (*viśvarūpa*) or a philosopher's stone (*cintāmaṇi*)[1]. Hence the difficulty of Its realization is being pointed out in the sentence; *kaḥ tam madanyaḥ jñātum arhati*, who apart from me can know It? Sleep is the cessation of the activities of the senses. The delimitation of Consciousness,[2] caused by the senses, ceases for a sleeping man. When the Self is in such a state (of sleep), Its consciousness being of a general character, It *yāti sarvataḥ*, seems to go, (to be present),

[1] A *viśvarūpa* gem appears possessed of diverse colours, and a *cintāmaṇi* assumes various aspects in accordance with the thought of its possessor.

[2] Then Consciousness has such limited expressions as, 'I am a man', 'I see a blue thing', and so on—A.G.

everywhere. When It is in a state of particularized consciousness, It, though really stationary by Its own nature, *dūram vrajati*, seems to travel far, in accordance with the movement of the mind etc., because It is conditioned by those mind etc. In reality, It continues here (in this body) only.

The text further shows how from the knowledge of the Self comes the elimination of grief as well:

अशरीरꣳ शरीरेष्वनवस्थेष्ववस्थितम् ।
महान्तं विभुमात्मानं मत्वा धीरो न शोचति ॥२२॥

22. Having meditated on the Self, as bodiless in the midst of bodies, as permanent in the midst of the impermanent, and as great and pervasive, the wise man does not grieve.

The Self in Its own nature, is like space; (having meditated on) that Self (as) *aśarīram*, unembodied—as that bodiless Self; *śarīreṣu*, in the midst of bodies—of gods, manes, human beings, etc.; (as) *avasthitam*, permanent, i. e. unchanging; *anavastheṣu*, in those that have no fixity—amidst the impermanent; and (having meditated) on the *mahāntam*, great—(and) lest the greatness be taken relatively, the text says—*vibhum*, pervasive; *ātmānam*, Self. The word *ātman* (Self) is used to show the nondistinction (of Brahman) from one's Self. The word *ātman* (Self) primarily means the indwelling Self. *Matvā*, having meditated—as 'I am this'—on this Self that is of this kind;

dhīraḥ, the wise man; *na śocati*, does not grieve. For grief cannot reasonably belong to a man of this kind who has known the Self.

The text says that though this Self is difficult to know, It can be known well through proper means:

नायमात्मा प्रवचनेन लभ्यो
न मेधया न बहुना श्रुतेन ।
यमेवैष वृणुते तेन लभ्य-
स्तस्यैष आत्मा विवृणुते तनूः स्वाम् ॥२३॥

23. This Self cannot be known through much study, nor through the intellect, nor through much hearing. It can be known through the Self alone that the aspirant prays to; this Self of that seeker reveals Its true nature.

Ayam ātmā, this Self; *na labhyaḥ*, is not to be attained, is not to be known; *pravacanena*, through the acquisition of many Vedas; and *na medhayā*, not through the intellect—through the power of grasping the meaning of texts; *na bahunā śrutena*, not through much hearing—alone. How is It then to be known? This is being said: *Yam eva*, that (Self) indeed which is his (i.e. aspirant's) own Self; which *eṣaḥ*, this one—the aspirant; *vṛṇute*, prays to; *tena*, by that—by that very Self which is the seeker (himself); the Self Itself is *labhyaḥ*, can be known, i.e. It becomes known to be such and such. The meaning is that to a desireless man who seeks for the Self alone, the Self becomes known of Its own accord.[1] How is It known? This is being said: *eṣaḥ*, this Self; *tasya*, of that seeker of the Self[2]; *vivṛṇute*, reveals; *svām*, Its own—Its real; *tanūm*, body, i.e. Its own nature.

There is this further fact:

नाविरतो दुश्चरितान्नाशान्तो नासमाहितः।
नाशान्तमानसो वाऽपि प्रज्ञानेनैनमाप्नुयात् ॥२४॥

24. One who has not desisted from bad conduct, whose senses are not under control, whose mind is not concentrated, whose mind is not free from anxiety (about the result of concentration), cannot attain this Self through knowledge.

Na aviratah, not one who has not desisted; *duścaritāt*, from bad conduct—from sinful works either prohibited, or not sanctioned by the Vedas and the Smṛtis; *na aśāntaḥ*, nor one whose senses are not controlled—one who has not turned away from the lure of the senses; *na asamāhitaḥ*, nor one whose mind is not concentrated—one whose mind is scattered; *na*, nor one whose mind may be concentrated, but still who is *aśāntamānasaḥ*, whose mind is not at rest, because of hankering for the result of concentration; *āpnuyāt*, can attain; *enam*, this Self, that is being considered; *prajñānena*, through knowledge—of Brahman. But the man who has desisted from

[1] Through Its grace. For other interpretations of the verse, see Mu. III. ii. 3.

[2] Some take *tasya* to mean 'to that seeker'.

bad conduct, as also from the lure of the senses, whose mind has become concentrated, and who is also free from anxiety about the results of concentration, and has a teacher, attains the aforesaid Self through knowledge. This is the idea.

यस्य ब्रह्म च क्षत्रं च उभे भवत ओदनः।
मृत्युर्यस्योपसेचनं क इत्था वेद यत्र सः ॥२५॥
इति काठकोपनिषदि प्रथमाध्याये द्वितीया वल्ली ॥

25. How can one know thus as to where It (the Self) is, for which both the Brāhmaṇa and the Ksatriya become food, and for which death takes the place of a curry?

But how can one, who is not of this kind, know the Self—the Self *yasya*, for which; *ubhe*, both; *brahma ca kṣatram ca*, the Brāhmaṇa and the Kṣatriya—though they are the upholders of all righteousness and the protectors of all; *bhavataḥ*, become; *odanaḥ*, food; *yasya*, for which Self; *mṛtyuḥ*, death—though it is the destroyer of all; (becomes) *upasecanam*, supplement to the food (like curry)—being unfit even to be a food; *kah*, who—being a man with a worldly intellect, and devoid of the disciplines described above; *veda*, knows; *itthā*, in this way—like the man endowed with the above mentioned disciplines; *yatra*, as to where[1]; *saḥ*, It—the Self (exists)?

[1] The Self, the eater—the destroyer of the universe—exists in Its own glory. Who knows It as such?

PART I

Canto III

The connection that this canto, beginning with *ṛtam pibantau*, has (with the earlier ones) is this: Knowledge and ignorance have been presented as possessed of diverse, opposite results; but they have not been ascertained properly (as regards their natures and means) together with their results. For the determination of this is called up the analogy of the chariot, inasmuch as this leads to easy comprehension. Thus also are presented two selves, for distinguishing between the attained and the attainer, and the goal and the goer.

ऋतं पिबन्तौ सुकृतस्य लोके
गुहां प्रविष्टौ परमे परार्धे (र्ध्ये) ।
छायातपौ ब्रह्मविदो वदन्ति
पञ्चाग्नयो ये च त्रिणाचिकेताः ॥१॥

1. The knowers of Brahman, the worshippers of the five fires,[1] and those who perform the Nāciketa sacrifice thrice, compare to shade and light, the two enjoyers of the inevitable results of work, who have entered within the body, into the cavity (of the heart) which is the supreme abode of the Most High (Brahman).

[1] Gārhapatya, Āhavanīya, Dakṣiṇāgni, Sabhya, and Āvasathya. Or heaven, cloud, earth, man, and woman—Bṛ. VI. ix-xiii.

Pibantau, two drinkers of; *ṛtam*, truth, i.e. the results of work (which is called truth) because of its inevitability. Of these two, one drinks—enjoys—the fruit of work, and not the other. Still both are called enjoyers, because of association with the enjoyer, on the analogy of the expression 'the possessors of the umbrella'.[1] *Sukṛtasya*, of what is done by oneself. This (word) is to be construed with *ṛtam*, mentioned earlier—(meaning thereby the drinkers of) the results of the work done by oneself. *Praviṣṭau*, (these) two have entered; *loke*, within this body; *guhām* (is the same as *guhāyām*), into the cavity, into the intellect. *Parame*, (means) in the supreme; it (i.e. the space within the heart) is supreme in comparison with the space outside (the cavity) circumscribed by the human body; *parārdhe*, into that which is the abode (*ardha*) of Brahman (*para*)—there, indeed, is the supreme Brahman perceived. So the meaning is that they two have entered into the supreme abode of Brahman, which is the space within the heart. And *brahmavidaḥ*, the knowers of Brahman; *vadanti*, speak of—these two; as different like *chāyātapau*, shade and light—because of (their) worldliness and freedom from worldliness. Not only those who have given up rites speak (thus), but also *pañcāgnayaḥ*, those who worship the five fires—i.e. the householders; *ca*, and also; those who are

[1] When a king with his retinue moves out in a procession with umbrellas, people say, '*Chatriṇaḥ yānti*—people with umbrellas are going', though most of the people in the procession do not possess umbrellas.

triṇāciketāḥ, the people by whom has been piled up thrice the fire called Nāciketa.

यः सेतुरीजानानामक्षरं ब्रह्म यत् परम् ।
अभयं तितीर्षतां पारं नाचिकेतꣳ शकेमहि ॥२॥

2. We have known that Nāciketa Fire, which is the bridge for the sacrificers, as also that which is the undecaying supreme Brahman beyond fear for those who want to cross over (the world).

Śakemahi, we were able to know as well as to pile up; *nāciketam*, the Nāciketa Fire (which is Virāṭ); *yaḥ*, who; is like a *setuḥ*, bridge—since it is calculated to lead beyond sorrow; *ījānānām*, for the sacrificers—the performers of rites. Moreover, that which is *abhayam*, the fearless; *akṣaram brahma*, the undecaying Brahman—which is the supreme resort of the knowers of Brahman and is called the Self; *pāram titīrṣatām*, for those who want to go to the shore—to the shore of the (sea of this) world—that also we succeeded to know. The meaning of the sentence is that both the inferior and the transcendental Brahman, which are the refuge of the knowers of rites and Brahman respectively, are worthy of realization. For these two, in fact, have been introduced in the verse, '*ṛtam pibantau*' etc.

For the sake of that one among these (two Selves), which has through limiting adjuncts become the transmigrating soul and is fit for knowledge and ignorance, a chariot, to attain either emancipation or the worldly state, is being imagined as a means to its reaching either.

आत्मानꣳ रथिनं विद्धि शरीरꣳ रथमेव तु ।
बुद्धिं तु सारथिं विद्धि मनः प्रग्रहमेव च ॥३॥

3. Know the (individual) self as the master of the chariot, and the body as the chariot. Know the intellect as the charioteer, and the mind as verily the bridle.

Of these, *viddhi*, know; *ātmānam*, the self—the enjoyer of the fruits of *karma*, which is the soul in the worldly state; as *rathinam*, the rider, the master of the chariot; *tu*, and; (know) *śarīram*, the body; as the *ratham*, the chariot—since the body is pulled by the organs which occupy the place of the horses tied to the chariot; *tu*, and; *viddhi*, know; *buddhim*, the intellect—characterized by determination; as *sārathim*, charioteer—since the body has the guiding intellect as its chief, just as the chariot has the guiding charioteer as its chief. All physical work, indeed, is generally directed by the intellect. Know *manaḥ*, the mind—characterized by volition, doubt, etc.; as *pragraham*, the bridle—for, just as the horses act when held in by the reins, similarly the organs such as ear etc. act when held in by the mind.

इन्द्रियाणि हयानाहुर्विषयाꣳ स्तेषु गोचरान् ।
आत्मेन्द्रियमनोयुक्तं भोक्तेत्याहुर्मनीषिणः ॥४॥

4. They call the organs the horses; the organs

having been imagined as horses, (know) the objects as the roads. The discriminating people call that Self the enjoyer when It is associated with body, organs, and mind.

Āhuḥ, they—those versed in calling up the imagery of the chariot—call; *indriyāṇi*, the organs—eye etc.; *hayān*, horses—because of the similarity of drawing the chariot and the body. *Teṣu*, those very organs having been imagined as horses; know, *viṣayān*, the objects—such as colour etc.; as *gocarān*, the roads. *Manīṣiṇaḥ*, the discriminating people; *āhuḥ*, call; *ātmendriyamanoyuktam*, the Self as associated with body, organs, and mind; as *bhoktā*, the enjoyer, the transmigrating soul. For the absolute Self can have no enjoyership; Its enjoyership is in fact created by the limiting adjuncts such as the intellect etc. Thus also there is another Vedic text which shows the non-enjoyership of the absolute (Self): 'It thinks, as it were, and shakes, as it were' etc. (Bṛ. IV. iii. 7). Only if this is so, does it become appropriate to attain the state of Viṣṇu (I. iii. 9) as one's own, through the analogy of the chariot which is going to be elaborated; but not otherwise, because one cannot transcend one's (true) nature.

This being so,

यस्त्वविज्ञानवान्भवत्ययुक्तेन मनसा सदा ।
तस्येन्द्रियाण्यवश्यानि दुष्टाश्वा इव सारथेः ॥५॥

5. But the organs of that intellect, which, being

ever associated with an uncontrolled mind, becomes devoid of discrimination, are unruly like the vicious horses of the charioteer.

Yaḥ tu, he, however, who—the charioteer called the intellect; *bhavati*, becomes; *avijñānavān*, unskilful—lacking in discrimination as regards engagement and disengagement, just as the other (real charioteer) is in conducting the chariot; being *sadā*, ever; associated *ayuktena manasā*, with an uncontrolled mind which is comparable to the bridle; *tasya*, his—of that incompetent intellect, i.e. of the driver; *indriyāṇi*, the organs—which are analogous to the horses; are *avaśyāni*, unruly, uncontrollable; *duṣṭāśvāḥ iva*, like the vicious horses; *sāratheḥ*, of the charioteer—of the other (real) driver.

यस्तु विज्ञानवान्भवति युक्तेन मनसा सदा ।
तस्येन्द्रियाणि वश्यानि सदश्वा इव सारथेः ॥६॥

6. But of that (intellect) which, being ever associated with a restrained mind, is endowed with discrimination, the organs are controllable like the good horses of the charioteer.

Yaḥ tu, but that (intellect), again, which is a charioteer opposed to the previous one; which *bhavati*, becomes; *vijñānavān*, skilful and possessed of discrimination; *yuktena manasā sadā*, being ever associated with a controlled mind—being endowed with a concentrated mind; *tasya*, of that (intellect); *indriyāṇi*, the organs—that are analogous to the horses; are *vaśyāni*, controllable—can be urged on or stopped; *sadaśvāḥ iva*, like the good horses; *sāratheḥ*, of the charioteer—of the other (real) driver.

This is the result that is being foretold for the aforesaid rider who has a non-discriminating intellect as his charioteer:

यस्त्वविज्ञानवान्भवत्यमनस्कः सदाऽशुचिः ।
न स तत्पदमाप्नोति संसारं चाधिगच्छति ॥७॥

7. But he, (that master of the chariot), does not attain that goal (through that intellect), who, being associated with a non-discriminating intellect and an uncontrollable mind, is ever impure; and he attains worldly existence.[1]

Yaḥ tu, but he (the soul, the master of the chariot) who; *avijñānavān bhavati*, is associated with a non-discriminating intellect; *amanaskaḥ*, whose mind is not under control; who is, because of that very reason, *aśuciḥ*, unclean; *sadā*, for ever; *saḥ*, that rider of the chariot; *na āpnoti*, does not attain—with the help of that charioteer (viz the intellect); *tat*, that—the aforesaid undecaying One; which is the supreme *padam*, goal. Not only does he not attain emancipation, but also *adhigacchati*, he reaches; *saṁsāram*, worldly existence—involving birth and death.

[1] Some translators take *yaḥ*, meaning the intellect, as the nominative of the first part, and *saḥ*, meaning the soul, as that of the second part.

यस्तु विज्ञानवान्भवति समनस्कः सदा शुचिः।
स तु तत्पदमाप्नोति यस्माद्भूयो न जायते ॥८॥

8. That (master of the chariot), however, who is associated with a discriminating intellect, and being endowed with a controlled mind, is ever pure, attains that goal from which he is not born again.

The other one, *yaḥ tu*, who, however; is *vijñānavān*, associated with a discriminating charioteer—i.e. the rider of the chariot who has knowledge; *samanaskaḥ*, who is possessed of a controlled mind; and who is for that very reason *sadā śuciḥ*, ever pure; *saḥ tu*, he however; *tat padam āpnoti*, attains that state; *yasmāt*, from which—becoming non-alienable from which acquired goal; he *na jāyate*, is not born—in the world; *bhūyaḥ*, again.

What is that goal? In answer the text says:

विज्ञानसारथिर्यस्तु मनः प्रग्रहवान्नरः।
सोऽध्वनः पारमाप्नोति तद्विष्णोः परमं पदम् ॥९॥

9. The man, however, who has as his charioteer a discriminating intellect, and who has under control the reins of the mind, attains the end of the road; and that is the highest place of Viṣṇu.

Yaḥ naraḥ tu, the man however, who, as described earlier; *vijñānasārathiḥ*, has a discriminating intellect as his charioteer; *manaḥ pragrahavān*, who has the mind as his reins—whose mind is controlled, who having a concentrated mind has become holy; *saḥ* (*naraḥ*), that man—that man of knowledge; *āpnoti*, reaches; *adhvanaḥ pāram*, the end of the road, i. e. the very supreme goal to be reached beyond the course of the world. He becomes free from all the worldly bondages. *Tat*, that; is *paramam padam*, the highest place, i.e. the very nature; *viṣṇoḥ*, of Viṣṇu —of the all-pervading Brahman, of the supreme Self who is called Vāsudeva[1]—which this man of knowledge attains.

Now this portion begins in order to show how the goal (i.e. Brahman), that is to be reached, is to be realized as the indwelling Self through an ascending gradation, from grossness to subtleness, commencing from the gross senses.

इन्द्रियेभ्यः परा ह्यर्था अर्थेभ्यश्च परं मनः ।
मनसस्तु परा बुद्धिर्बुद्धेरात्मा महान्परः ॥१०॥

10. The sense-objects are higher than the senses, and the mind is higher than the sense-objects; but the intellect is higher than the mind, and the Great Soul is higher than the intellect.

Now, then, the senses are gross. The *arthāḥ*, sense-objects, by which those senses were created for their (i.e. of the sense-objects) own revelation; are certainly *parāḥ*, higher—subtler, more pervasive,

[1] He who provides dwelling place (*vāsa*) for all in Himself, is *vāsu*. *Deva* is effulgent, i.e. self-luminous. He is both *vāsu* and *deva*.

and are their inner selves; *indriyebhyaḥ*, than those senses—which are their own effects (the sense-organs having been created from sense-objects for perceiving them). *Arthebhyaḥ ca*, as compared with even those sense-objects; *manaḥ*, the ·mind; is *param*, higher—more subtle, pervasive, and is their inner self. By the word *manaḥ* is indicated the elements in their rudimentary subtle form (*tanmātras*) which are the material cause of the mind, for they are the originators of volition and conjecture. *Manasaḥ* (*api*), as compared with even the mind; *buddhiḥ*, the intellect; is *parā*, higher—subtler, more pervasive, and is their inner self. By the word *buddhiḥ*, is denoted the rudimentary elements (*tanmātras*) which are the source of determination etc. *Buddheḥ*, as compared with the intellect; *mahān ātmā*, the Great Soul (is higher); it is *ātmā*, the soul, because it is the innermost principle of the intelligence of all beings, and it is *mahān*, great, because it is the most pervasive of all. The principle called Hiraṇyagarbha, which was born before all, from the Unmanifested (Māyā), and which consists of both intelligence and activity, is called the Great Soul that is *paraḥ*, higher, than the intellect.

महतः परमव्यक्तमव्यक्तात्पुरुषः परः ।
पुरुषान्न परं किंचित्सा काष्ठा सा परा गतिः ॥११॥

11. The Unmanifested is higher than Mahat; the Puruṣa is higher than the Unmanifested. There is nothing higher than the Puruṣa. He is the culmination, He is the highest goal.

Mahataḥ, as compared (even) with Mahat (the Great Soul); *param*, higher—subtler, the inner self, and the most pervasive; is *avyaktam*, the Unmanifested—that which is the seed of the whole universe, the essence of unmanifested name and form, the state of aggregation of all powers of causes and effects,[1] called by such names as *avyakta* (Unmanifested), *avyākṛta* (Unevolved), *ākāśa* (Space), etc., resting on the supreme Self through and through like the potentiality of a banyan tree in a tiny banyan seed.[2] *Avyaktāt*, as compared with that *avyakta*[3]; (the Puruṣa is) *paraḥ*, higher—subtler and greater, being the cause of all the causes and the inmost self of all—and therefore too, He is called *puruṣaḥ*, because He fills up everything. Ruling out the possibility of anything being higher than Him, the text says, *puruṣāt na param kiṁ cit*, there is nothing higher than the Puruṣa. Since there is no other substance beyond the Puruṣa who is a mass of pure consciousness, therefore, *sā*, He, the Puruṣa; is *kāṣṭhā*, the acme, the culmination—of subtleness, greatness, and inwardness, as Self. Here, indeed, culminate all subtleness etc., commencing from the

[1] During cosmic dissolution.

[2] 'As the seed, with the potentiality of the tree, is but a single entity, without a second, similarly Brahman, too, as possessed of the power of Māyā, is not a dual entity.'—A. G.

[3] That has no individuality when ascertained from the point of view of existence etc. It is the cause of the whole manifested world. Since it is dependent on the supreme Self, the latter is indirectly called the cause. But in reality the Self is not the cause, because It is not subject to mutation.

senses. And hence this is *parā gatiḥ*, the supreme goal—of all travellers, all individual souls that transmigrate; because the Smṛti says, 'Going where they do not return.' (G. VIII. 21; XV. 6)

Objection: Is it not a fact that if there is going, there shall be coming as well? How is it then said, 'from which he is not born again'? (I. iii. 8)

Answer: That is no fault. Since He is the indwelling Self of all, the fact of realizing Him is figuratively spoken of as attaining Him. And that He is the indwelling Self is shown through His being higher than the senses, the mind, and the intellect. He who is a traveller goes, indeed, to something that is unattained, non-immanent, and non-Self; but not contrariwise. Thus there is the Vedic text: 'Those who want to get beyond the ways (of the world), do not walk on roads', etc. (Iti. 18) Thus also is being shown that He is the indwelling Self of all:

एष सर्वेषु भूतेषु गूढोऽऽत्मा न प्रकाशते ।
दृश्यते त्वग्र्यया बुद्ध्या सूक्ष्मया सूक्ष्मदर्शिभिः ॥१२॥

12. He is hidden in all beings, and hence He does not appear as the Self (of all). But by the seers of subtle things, He is seen through a pointed and fine intellect.

Eṣaḥ, this one—this Puruṣa; *sarveṣu bhūteṣu*, in all creatures—from Brahmā to a clump of grass; *gūḍhaḥ*, is hidden—though He has such activities as hearing, seeing, etc., yet He is covered by *avidyā*, i.e. Māyā.[1] Thus, since He is the *ātmā*, the Self (of all); *na prakāśate*, (He) does not appear as the Self of anyone.[2] Alas, how unfathomable, inscrutable, and variegated is this Māyā, that every creature, though in reality identical with the supreme Entity, and is instructed as such, does not grasp the fact 'I am the supreme Self', while even without being told, he accepts as his Self the non-selves, viz the aggregate of body and senses, under the idea 'I am the son of such a one', though these (latter) are objects of perception to oneself (and are hence not his selves) like pots etc.! Verily, it is because of being deluded by the Māyā of the supreme Being that every man moves again and again (through birth and death). There is this Smṛti on this point: 'I am not revealed to all, being veiled by my Yoga-Māyā (i. e. the illusion born of the congress of the *guṇas*), etc. (G. VII. 25)

Objection: Is it not contradictory to say, 'Having realized It, the intelligent man does not grieve' (II. i.4) and 'He does not appear'?

Answer: This is not so. Since He is not known to a man whose intellect has not been purified, it is said, 'He does not appear'. *Tu* (but); *dṛśyate*, (He) is seen; through the purified (intellect)—*agryayā*, through the pointed (intellect); that (intellect) which is like a

[1] The very word *avidyā* (ignorance) suggests that it is removable by *vidyā* (knowledge); and Māyā (cosmic illusion) suggests that it is unreal.

[2] The Self, as such, cannot be the content of any conventional idea.

point (*agra*) is *agryā*; through that, i. e. through that (intellect) which is associated with concentration; *sūkṣmayā*, through the subtle (intellect) that is engaged in ascertaining subtle things.[1] By whom? *Sūkṣmadarśibhiḥ*, by the seers of subtle things. The seers are those who have become skilled in penetrating into the subtlest thing through their perception of an ascending order of subtleness by following the process as indicated in the text, 'The sense-objects are higher than the senses', etc. (I. iii. 10) By them, i.e. by the wise people.

The means for His attainment is being stated:

यच्छेद्वाङ्मनसी प्राज्ञस्तद्यच्छेज्ज्ञान आत्मनि ।
ज्ञानमात्मनि महति नियच्छेत्तद्यच्छेच्छान्त आत्मनि ॥१३॥

13. The discriminating man should merge the (organ of) speech into the mind; he should merge that (mind) into the intelligent self; he should merge the intelligent self into the Great Soul; he should merge the Great Soul into the peaceful Self.

Prājñaḥ, the discriminating man; *yacchet*, should merge. What (should he merge)? *Vāk*, i.e. *vācam*,

[1] 'When the mind becomes concentrated through the perfection of meditation and thus becomes helpful, then from the *mahāvākya* (great saying—*Thou art That*) associated with that mind, there arises such a conviction as "I am Brahman." On that intellectual pattern is revealed the reality of Brahman; and this is conventionally referred to as the self-revealed immediate perception of Brahman.'—A.G.

the organ of speech, (i.e. all the organs), *vāk* being used suggestively for all organs. Where? *Manasī*, into the mind; the use of the word with a long *ī* is a Vedic licence. *Tat*, that mind, again; *yacchet*, he should merge; *jñāne ātmani*, into the intellect—bright by nature—which is their self; as the intellect pervades the organs, beginning with the mind, it is their self, their innermost principle. *Jñānam*, the intellect; *niyacchet*, he should dissolve; *mahati ātmani*, in the Great Soul—the First Born (Hiraṇyagarbha). The idea is that he should make the intelligence as clear in its nature as is the First Born. And that Great Soul again, *yacchet*, he should sink; *śānte*, into the peaceful—whose nature does not admit of any distinction, which is unchangeable; (into that peaceful) *ātmani*, Self—into the real Self which is within all and is the witness of all the modifications of the intellect.

Just as the water in a mirage, the snake on a rope, and dirt in the sky, are eliminated through the perception of the real nature of the mirage, rope, and the sky, similarly by dissolving in the Puruṣa—the Self—through the knowledge of the true nature of one's own Self, all that is projected by unreal ignorance, which is characterized by action, instrument, and result, and which is but constituted by the three—name, form, and action—one becomes established in the Self and peaceful in mind, and he has his goal achieved. Since this is so, therefore, for the sake of realizing this—

उत्तिष्ठत जाग्रत

प्राप्य वरान्निबोधत ।

क्षुरस्य धारा निशिता दुरत्यया
दुर्गं पथस्तत्कवयो वदन्ति ॥१४॥

14. Arise, awake, and learn by approaching the excellent ones. The wise ones describe that path to be as impassable as a razor's edge, which, when sharpened, is difficult to tread on.

You creatures, who are sleeping in ignorance that has no beginning, *uttiṣṭhata*, arise, turn towards the knowledge of the Self; *jāgrata*, awake—put an end to the sleep of ignorance which is terrible by nature, and is the seed of all evil. How (to put an end to it)? *Prāpya*, approaching; *varān*, the adorable ones, the excellent teachers—who know that (Self); *nibodhata*, learn—understand the all-pervading Self, taught by them, as 'I am that'. The Upaniṣad says out of compassion, like a mother, that this should not be neglected, for the thing to be known is comprehensible by a very fine intellect. With what can that fine intellect be compared? This is being said: *Dhārā*, the edge; *kṣurasya*, of a razor; *niśitā*, being sharpened; becomes, *duratyayā*, such as can be passed over with great difficulty, impassable. As that razor is difficult to walk on with the feet, similarly, *kavayaḥ*, the intelligent people; *vadanti*, describe; *pathaḥ* (should rather be *panthānam*), the path—consisting in the knowledge of Reality; (as) *durgam*, impassable, i.e. hard to attain. The idea is that since the object to be known is very subtle, they speak of the path of knowledge leading to it as impassable.

How is the thing to be known very subtle? That is

being said: Now, then, this earth is gross, developed as it is by (the principles of) sound, touch, colour, taste, and smell; and it is an object of perception to all the senses. So also is the body. Here a gradation of subtleness, pervasiveness, purity, permanence, etc. is noticed in water etc., through the elimination of the attributes of smell etc., one by one, till one reaches *ākāśa*[1] (space). Therefore, what need is there to speak of the unsurpassable subtleness etc. of that in which do not exist those attributes—beginning with smell and ending with sound—that are the causes of grossness. This is what the Upanisad shows:

अशब्दमस्पर्शमरूपमव्ययं
तथाऽरसं नित्यमगन्धवच्च यत् ।
अनाद्यनन्तं महतः परं ध्रुवं
निचाय्य तन्मृत्युमुखात् प्रमुच्यते ॥१५॥

15. One becomes freed from the jaws of death by knowing That which is soundless, touchless, colourless, undiminishing, and also tasteless, eternal, odourless, without beginning, and without end, distinct from Mahat, and ever constant.

[1] Earth is possessed of five qualities—smell, taste, colour, touch, and sound; water consists of the four qualities beginning from taste; fire of the next three; air of the next two; and space of the last one. It is difficult to translate the word *ākāśa*. *Vedāntasāra* defines it as the element that provides space and has sound as its quality.

Yat, that which—is described as; *aśabdam*, soundless; *asparśam*, touchless; *arūpam*, colourless; *avyayam*, undiminishing; *tathā*, and also; *arasam*, tasteless; *nityam*, eternal—that is the undecaying Brahman. That which is possessed of sound etc., diminishes. But this one, being soundless etc., is *avyayam*—It does not diminish, does not decay; and because of this, It is eternal. Whatever decays is non-eternal; but this one does not decay, therefore it is permanent. For this further reason, too, It is eternal: that which has no *ādi* (beginning), cause, is *anādi*, beginningless. That which has a cause, is impermanent, because it is an effect and it merges into its cause, as for instance earth etc. But this one being the cause of all, is not the effect; and because It is not an effect, It is eternal; It has no cause into which It can merge. Similarly, *anantam*, infinite—that which has no end, no effect. As the plantain etc. are seen to be impermanent after yielding their products in the form of fruits etc., not even in that way has Brahman any finitude; hence too, It is eternal. *Mahataḥ*, from the principle Mahat, called *buddhi*, intelligence; It is *param*, distinct, by nature—for It is the witness of all, being eternal Consciousness; and It is Brahman, being the Self of all beings. For it has been already said, 'He is hidden in all beings', etc. (I. iii. 12) And It is *dhruvam*, changelessly constant, whose eternality is not relative like that of the earth etc. *Nicāyya*, realizing; *tat*, that Self—the Self that is the Brahman of this kind; *pramucyate*, one gets freed from—detached from; *mṛtyumukhāt*, from the jaws, the grasp, of Death—which consists of ignorance, desire, and action.

For the sake of eulogizing the knowledge under discussion the Upaniṣad says:

नाचिकेतमुपाख्यानं मृत्युप्रोक्तꣳ सनातनम् ।
उक्त्वा श्रुत्वा च मेधावी ब्रह्मलोके महीयते ॥१६॥

16. Relating and hearing this eternal anecdote—as received by Naciketā and as told by Death—the intelligent man becomes glorified in the region that is Brahman.

Uktvā, relating—to Brāhmaṇas; *ca*, and; *śrutvā*, hearing—from teachers; this *sanātanam upākhyānam*, eternal anecdote—eternal because it is Vedic; (that was) *nāciketam*, received by Naciketā; (and) *mṛtyuproktam*, told by Death; *medhāvī*, the intelligent man; *mahīyate*, becomes glorified—i.e. he becomes adorable by becoming identified with Brahman; *brahmaloke*, in the region of Brahman that is identical with Brahman Itself.

य इमं परमं गुह्यं श्रावयेद् ब्रह्मसंसदि ।
प्रयतः श्राद्धकाले वा तदानन्त्याय कल्पते ।
तदानन्त्याय कल्पत इति ॥१७॥

इति काठकोपनिषदि प्रथमाध्याये तृतीया वल्ली ॥

17. Should anyone, after purification, get this highest secret recited before an assembly of Brāhmaṇas, or at the time of the ceremonies for the dead, (then) that (ceremony) becomes conducive to eternal result.

Should *yaḥ*, anyone; *prayataḥ*, after becoming purified; *idam śrāvayet*, get this text recited—verbatim, as also with explanation; (that is) *paramam guhyam*, the greatest secret; *brahmasamsadi*, in an assemblage of Brāhmaṇas; *vā*, or; get it recited *śrāddhakāle*, at the time of the ceremonies for the dead, to the Brāhmaṇas seated for the feast; (then) *tat*, that—funeral ceremony, of that man; *kalpate*, becomes conducive; *ānantyāya*, to eternal result. The repetition is for concluding the Part.

PART II

Canto I

It has been stated, 'He is hidden in all beings, and hence He does not appear as the Self (of all). But He is seen through a pointed and fine intellect.' (I. iii. 12) What again is the obstacle to this pointed intellect because of which there is an absence of that intellect and the Self is not seen? This canto is begun to show the cause of that non-perception.[1] For only when the cause that bars the good is known, can effort be made to remove it and not otherwise:

पराञ्चि खानि व्यतृणत् स्वयम्भू-
स्तस्मात्पराङ्पश्यति नान्तरात्मन् ।
कश्चिद्धीरः प्रत्यगात्मानमैक्ष-
दावृत्तचक्षुरमृतत्वमिच्छन् ॥१॥

1. The self-existent Lord destroyed the outgoing senses. Therefore, one sees the outer things and not the inner Self. A rare discriminating man, desiring immortality, turns his eyes away and then sees the indwelling Self.

Parāñci, outgoing; by the word *khāni* (*kha* meaning an orifice, cavity) are referred to the senses such

[1] This is according to the reading *tadadarśana*. The other reading is *taddarśana*, which gives the opposite meaning.

as ear etc.[1], which are suggestively indicated by it. They surely proceed outward for revealing their objects, sound etc. Since they are of such a nature, He *vyatṛṇat*, afflicted, i. e. killed these. Who is He (that did so)? *Svayambhūḥ*, the Great Lord—who (*bhū*) exists ever, and (*svayam*, by Himself) on His own right, and is not subject to anything else. (Since He injured them), *tasmāt*, therefore; the perceiver (the individual) *paśyati*, sees, perceives; *parāk*, the outer—sounds etc., which are the non-Self and exist as external things; *na antarātman*, i.e. *na antarātmānam*, but (sees) not the inner Self. Though such is the nature of man, yet like reversing the current of a river *kaḥ cit dhīraḥ*, some (rare) discriminating man (sees); *pratyagātmānam*, the indwelling Self. That which is *pratyak*, in the interior, and at the same time *ātmā*, the Self, is the *pratyagātmā*. In common usage the word *ātmā* conventionally means only the individual soul, and not anything else. From the point of etymology, too, the word *ātmā* has that very sense. For in the Smṛti the derivation of the word is given thus: 'Since It pervades, absorbs, and enjoys (all) objects in the world, and since from It the world derives its continuous existence, therefore, It is called the *ātmā*.' (L. P. I. LXX. 96) That indwelling Self—one's own reality—one *aikṣat*, saw, i.e. sees, for in the Vedas there is no regularity about the tenses. How one sees is being stated: (Becoming) *āvṛttacakṣuḥ*, having one's eyes covered—having one's eye, i.e. the group of organs beginning with the ear,

[1] Actually meaning the senses—of hearing, sight, etc.

turned away from all sense-objects. Such a one, who is purified thus, sees the indwelling Self. For it is not possible for the same person to be engaged in the thought of sense-objects and to have the vision of the Self as well. Why, again, does the discriminating man check his natural propensity thus through great effort and then realize the Self? This is the answer: *Icchan*, desiring—for oneself; *amṛtatvam*, immortality—one's own unchanging nature.

पराचः कामाननुयन्ति बाला-
स्ते मृत्योर्यन्ति विततस्य पाशम्।
अथ धीरा अमृतत्वं विदित्वा
ध्रुवमध्रुवेष्विह न प्रार्थयन्ते ॥२॥

2. The unintelligent people follow the external desires. They get entangled in the snares of the widespread death. Therefore, the discriminating people, having known what true immortality is in the midst of impermanent things, do not pray for anything here.

Now then, the natural tendency to perceive only outwardly the things that are not the Self, is the cause of obstruction of the vision of the Self and it is ignorance, since it is opposed to that (vision). And there is that thirst for the enjoyment of those very outer things, whether seen or unseen, which are presented by ignorance. Those whose vision of the Self is obstructed by those two—ignorance and thirst—those *bālāḥ*, men of little intelligence; *anuyanti*, follow; only *parācaḥ kāmān*, the external desirable things. *Te*, they; because of that reason, *yanti*, get entangled in; *pāśam*, the snares — those by which one is bound, consisting in the association with, or dissociation from, the body, senses, etc.; *vitatasya*, of that which is vast, spread everywhere; *mṛtyoḥ*, of death — of the group of ignorance, desire, and action. The meaning is that they are constantly subject to birth, death, old age, disease, and a mass of such other multifarious evils. Since this is so, *atha*, hence; *dhīrāḥ*, the discriminating people; *viditvā*, having known; *amṛtatvam*, immortality — which consists in continuing in the true state of the indwelling Self; as the *dhruvam*, sure thing; for the immortality of the gods and others is unstable, whereas this immortality consisting in continuing in the true state of the indwelling Self is stable, as is supported by the text, 'It neither increases nor decreases through work.' (Bṛ. IV. iv. 23) Having known the constant and unshakable immortality which is of this kind, having ascertained it from *adhruveṣu*, amidst all impermanent things; the knowers of Brahman *na prārthayante*, do not pray for — anything; *iha*, in this world, that is full of evil; because all this is opposed to the vision of the innermost Self. The idea is that they inevitably rise above the desires for progeny, wealth, and worlds (of enjoyment).

How is that known, by realizing which the men of enlightenment do not pray for anything else? This is being said:

येन रूपं रसं गन्धं शब्दान् स्पर्शांश्च मैथुनान् ।
एतेनैव विजानाति किमत्र परिशिष्यते । एतद्वै तत् ॥३॥

3. What remains here (unknowable to this Self) through which very Self people perceive colour, taste, smell, sound, touch, and sexual pleasure? This indeed is that (Self asked for by Naciketā).

Yena, that by which—by the Self which is consciousness by nature; all people *vijānāti*, know clearly; *rūpam*, colour; *rasam*, taste; *gandham*, smell; *śabdam*, sound; *sparśān*, touch; *ca*, and; *maithunān*, pleasurable sensations from sex.

Objection: May it not be argued that the idea, 'I know through the Self which is distinct from the body etc.', is not familiar to anyone? Rather all people experience thus: 'I, who am the combination of the body etc., know.'

Answer: But this is not so. Since even the aggregate of body etc. is substantially indistinguishable from (knowable objects like) sound etc., and hence it, too, is equally a knowable, it cannot reasonably be the knower. If the aggregate of body etc., though constituted by colour etc., can perceive colour etc., then the external colour etc. may as well know each other, as also their own individual feature. But this does not tally with facts. Therefore, just as that through which iron burns (anything) is (inferred to be) fire, similarly people perceive colour and other attributes, in the form of the body etc., *etena eva*, through this only—through the Self which is consciousness by nature and which is distinct from the body etc. *Kim*, what; *atra*, in this world; *pariśiṣyate*, remains, which is unknowable to the Self? Nothing remains, but everything can certainly be known through the Self. The Self to which nothing can remain unknown is omniscient. *Etat vai tat*, this (Self) indeed is that. What is that? That which was asked for by Naciketā, about which even the gods had doubts, which is different from virtue etc., which is the highest state of Viṣṇu, and beyond which there is nothing. That very thing, which is described thus, is comprehended here. This is the idea.

Thinking that the Self, being subtle, is difficult to know, the text states the same idea over and over again:

स्वप्नान्तं जागरितान्तं चोभौ येनानुपश्यति ।
महान्तं विभुमात्मानं मत्वा धीरो न शोचति ॥४॥

4. Having realized the great and all-pervading Self, through which a man perceives the objects in both the sleep and the waking states, a wise man does not grieve.

Yena, that—the Self—through which; a man *anupaśyati*, perceives; *svapnāntam*, the content of sleep, i.e. the objects in sleep; similarly *jāgaritāntam*, the content of the waking state, the objects in the waking state; *ubhau*, both—the sleep and waking objects. All this is to be explained as before.[1]

[1] The objection that can be raised with regard to the Self's being the real knower is to be met as in II. i. 3.

Matvā, realizing; that *mahāntam vibhum ātmānam*, great and all-pervading Self; having directly known It as identified with oneself thus, 'I am the supreme Self'; *dhīraḥ*, the wise man; *na śocati*, does not grieve.

य इमं मध्वदं वेद आत्मानं जीवमन्तिकात् ।
ईशानं भूतभव्यस्य न ततो विजुगुप्सते । एतद्वै तत् ॥५॥

5. Anyone who knows proximately[1] this Self—the enjoyer of the fruits of works, the supporter of life etc.—as the lord of the past and the future, does not want to save (the Self) just because of that (knowledge). This indeed is that.

Moreover, *yaḥ*, anyone who; *veda*, knows; *antikāt*, proximately; *imam*, this; *ātmānam*, Self; *jīvam*, the sustainer of the whole lot of vital force etc.; *madhvadam*, the enjoyer of the fruits of works; as *īśānam*, the ruler; *bhūtabhavyasya*, of past and future—of all the three times; *tataḥ*, after that—after that knowledge; *na vijugupsate*, does not want to save (the Self)—because he has attained fearlessness. One wants to save the Self so long as one is in the midst of fear and considers the Self to be impermanent. But when one knows the eternal, non-dual Self, then who would wish to save what or from where? *Etat vai tat* is to be explained as before.

It is being shown that the indwelling Self, which has been identified with God, is the Self of all:

[1] As non-different from oneself.

यः पूर्वं तपसो जातमद्भ्यः पूर्वमजायत ।
गुहां प्रविश्य तिष्ठन्तं यो भूतेभिर्व्यपश्यत । एतद्वै तत् ॥६॥

6. He sees this very aforesaid Brahman who sees the First Born (Hiraṇyagarbha)—born before the five elements from Consciousness (Brahman)—as existing in the cavity of the heart in the midst of body and senses, after having entered there.

Yaḥ, anyone—who being desirous of freedom; (*vyapaśyata*, sees) *pūrvam jātam*, the First Born—Hiraṇyagarbha; *yaḥ*, who; *ajāyata*, was born; *pūrvam*, earlier. Earlier than what? That is being said: *Adbhyaḥ*, than water; the idea is that He was earlier than the five elements inclusive of water, and not merely earlier than water. *Tapasaḥ*, (born) from Brahman, characterized by consciousness etc. Anyone who (sees) that First Born, who after having created the bodies of gods etc., (and) *praviśya guhām*, having entered into the cavity of the heart, of everybody; *tiṣṭhantam*, remains in existence; *bhūtebhiḥ*, in association with the elements—in the midst of body and senses, perceiving sound etc.; *yaḥ vyapaśyata*, i.e. *paśyati*, anyone who sees thus, he sees; *etat*, this very one,[1] Brahman, that is under discussion.

या प्राणेन संभवत्यदितिर्देवतामयी ।
गुहां प्रविश्य तिष्ठन्तीं या भूतेभिर्व्यजायत । एतद्वै तत् ॥७॥

[1] As an ornament made of gold continues to be gold, so is Hiraṇyagarbha nothing but Brahman.

7. He (sees) that very Brahman (who sees) that Aditi, comprising all the deities, who takes birth as Hiraṇyagarbha, who is manifested in association with the elements, and who is seated in the cavity of the heart, after entering there.

Furthermore, *yā aditiḥ*, that Aditi—so called because of enjoying (*adana*) all such things as sound; who is *devatāmayī*, who comprises all the deities; (and) who *sambhavati*, takes birth; *prāṇena*, as Hiraṇyagarbha—from the supreme Brahman. The portion 'He who sees that Aditi as existing in the cavity of the heart after having entered there', is to be explained as before. That very Aditi is being distinguished: *yā*, which; *bhūtebhiḥ*, as associated with the elements; *vyajāyata*, took birth, i.e. was created.

अरण्योर्निहितो जातवेदा गर्भ इव सुभृतो गर्भिणीभिः।
दिवे दिव ईड्यो जागृवद्भिर्हविष्मद्भिर्मनुष्येभिरग्निः।
एतद्वै तत् ॥८॥

8. The sacrificial Fire lodged in two fire-producing pieces of wood, (as also the Fire lodged in the hearts of Yogis) that is well protected—just as much as the foetus by pregnant women—and the Fire that is adorable every day by vigilant men with oblation (and contemplation)—that Fire too is but this Brahman.

Besides, that *jātavedāḥ*, Fire; which in the context of a sacrifice, is *nihitaḥ*, lodged; *araṇyoḥ*, in the upper and lower pieces of wood (by rubbing which fire is produced); which, again, as the eater of all oblations, is (lodged) in the individual person (as Virāṭ, in the heart); and which is *subhṛtaḥ*, well protected—by the men of contemplation; *garbhaḥ iva*, just as the foetus—is well protected; *garbhinībhiḥ*, by pregnant women—by partaking of food, drink, etc. that are not improper. The meaning is that, just as in the world the foetus is well protected, similarly it (i.e. the Fire) is protected by the priests and the meditators. Moreover, that *agniḥ*, Fire; which is *īḍyaḥ*, laudable and adorable—by sacrificers and meditators, in the sacrifices and the hearts; *dive*, *dive*, every day; *jāgṛvadbhiḥ*, by the sleepless, i.e. the vigilant; *manuṣyebhiḥ*, i.e. *manuṣyaiḥ*, by men; *haviṣmadbhiḥ*, who are possessed of oblations, e.g. ghee, as also possessed of meditation and contemplation; *tat*, that Fire; *etat vai*, is this only—the Brahman that is being discussed.

यतश्चोदेति सूर्योऽस्तं यत्र च गच्छति ।
तं देवाः सर्वे अर्पितास्तदु नात्येति कश्चन । एतद्वै तत् ॥९॥

9. On that, from which the sun rises and in which it sets, are fixed all the deities. None ever transcends that. This indeed is that.

Moreover, *yataḥ ca*, that from which—from which Prāṇa (i.e. Hiraṇyagarbha); *udeti*, rises; *sūryaḥ*, the sun; *yatra*, where, in which Prāṇa itself; it *astam gacchati*, sets—day after day; *tam*, on that—on the Prāṇa which is the Self; *sarve devāḥ*, all the gods—Fire and others in the divine context, and speech etc. in the personal context; *arpitāḥ*, are fixed—like spokes on the nave of a chariot wheel—during the period of existence (of the universe). He (that Prāṇa), too, is Brahman. This is that all pervading Brahman. *Tat u*, that indeed; *na kaḥ cana*, nobody—whosoever; *atyeti*, transcends—ceasing to be identified with It, becomes something other than that. This indeed is that.

The following verse is there to counteract the doubt that may arise in anybody's mind that the entity which exists in all beings from Brahmā down to the immovable, and appears as non-Brahman owing to those particular limiting adjuncts, is (an individual soul) different from the supreme Brahman, and is subject to birth and death:

यदेवेह तदमुत्र यदमुत्र तदन्विह ।
मृत्योः स मृत्युमाप्नोति य इह नानेव पश्यति ॥१०॥

10. What indeed is here, is there; what is there, is here likewise. He who sees as though there is difference here, goes from death to death.

Yat eva iha, what, indeed, is here—that entity which, being associated with limiting adjuncts, viz the body and senses (i.e. as existing here in the individual), appears to the ignorant to be possessed of worldly attributes; *tat*, that—very entity, established in Its own reality, is; *amutra*, there—(existing in Its causal condition as) Brahman which is by nature a mass of constant consciousness and is devoid of all worldly attributes. And *yat amutra*, that which is there (in the causal condition), established in Itself; *tat*, that very thing; *iha anu*, (is) here likewise—appearing diversely in conformity with the limiting adjuncts such as name and form, body and senses; It is nothing else. This being so, *yaḥ*, anyone who—being deluded by ignorance that consists in seeing differences that are natural to the limiting adjuncts; *paśyati*, sees, perceives; *iha*, here—in Brahman, which is not a plurality; *nānā iva*, as though there is difference—feels such differences as, 'I am different from the supreme Self, and the supreme Brahman is different from me'; *saḥ*, he; *āpnoti*, gets; *mṛtyoḥ mṛtyum*, death after death, he becomes subject to repeated birth and death. Therefore, one should not perceive like that; one should perceive thus: 'I am, indeed, Brahman which is homogeneous consciousness and which pervades everything through and through like space.' This is the meaning of the sentence.

मनसैवेदमाप्तव्यं नेह नानाऽस्ति किंचन।
मृत्योः स मृत्युं गच्छति य इह नानेव पश्यति ॥११॥

11. This is to be attained through the mind indeed. There is no diversity here whatsoever. He who sees as though there is difference here, goes from death to death.

Before attaining the knowledge of unity, *idam*, this—Brahman which is homogeneous; *āptavyam*, is to be attained, as identical with the Self, there being nothing else existing; *manasā*, through the mind—which is purified by the teacher and the scriptures. And since ignorance that presents diversity ceases on this attainment, (therefore) *iha*, here—in the Brahman; *nānā*, diversity; *kiṁcana*, even so little; *na asti*, does not exist. On the other hand, *yaḥ*, he who—does not give up his vision of ignorance that is comparable to darkness; (and) *nānā iva paśyati*, sees as though there is diversity; *saḥ*, he; *mṛtyoḥ mṛtyum gacchati*, does (indeed) go from death to death, even by superimposing the slightest difference. This is the idea.

The Upaniṣad again speaks of that very Brahman which is being discussed:

अङ्गुष्ठमात्रः पुरुषो मध्य आत्मनि तिष्ठति।
ईशानं भूतभव्यस्य न ततो विजुगुप्सते। एतद्वै तत् ॥१२॥

12. The Being (Purusa), of the size of a thumb, resides in the body. Knowing Him as the ruler of the past and the future, one does not want, by virtue of that knowledge, to save the Self. This indeed is that.

Aṅguṣṭhamātraḥ, of the size of a thumb: the lotus of the heart is of the size of a thumb; (and) as conditioned by the internal organ existing in the space within the lotus of the heart, (the Self) has the size of a thumb, just like space existing in a section of a bamboo that is of the size of a thumb. *Purusah* means He by whom everything is filled. Knowing

Him, who *tiṣṭhati*, stays; *madhye ātmani*, in the body; as the *īśānam*[1] *bhūtabhavyasya*, the ruler of the past and the future—of the three times. (The portion) *na tataḥ* etc. is to be explained as before (II. i. 5).

अङ्गुष्ठमात्रः पुरुषो ज्योतिरिवाधूमकः ।
ईशानो भूतभव्यस्य स एवाद्य स उ श्वः । एतद्वै तत् ॥१३॥

13. The Puruṣa, who is of the size of a thumb, is like a light without smoke. He is the ruler of the past and the future. He exists today, and He will exist tomorrow. This indeed is that.

Moreover, *aṅguṣṭhamātraḥ puruṣaḥ*, the Puruṣa (the all-pervasive entity) of the size of a thumb; is *jyotiḥ iva adhūmakaḥ*, like a smokeless light. *Adhūmakaḥ* should rather be *adhūmakam*, since it qualifies *jyotiḥ* which is neuter). He, who is perceived as such by the Yogis in their hearts, is the *īśānaḥ bhūtabhavyasya*, lord of the past and the future. *Saḥ*, He, the eternal and unchanging; exists *adya*, now, in all beings; *u*, and; *saḥ*, He; will exist *śvaḥ*, even tomorrow. The idea is that none equals Him now, nor will any be born in future (to do so). Though one of the alternatives, viz 'Some say that He does not exist (after death)' (I. i. 20), cannot logically arise, yet hereby it is refuted by the Upaniṣad itself in its own words, and so also is dismissed the theory of momentary existence.

[1] The alternative reading is *īśāno bhūtabhavyasya*.

The Upanisad again presents a refutation of the perception of difference with regard to Brahman:

यथोदकं दुर्गे वृष्टं पर्वतेषु विधावति।
एवं धर्मान् पृथक् पश्यंस्तानेवानुविधावति ॥१४॥

14. As water rained on an inaccessible height gets dispersed on (lower) hilly regions, similarly, one who perceives the selves differently, runs after them only.

Yathā, as; *udakam*, water; *vrṣṭam*, poured; *durge*, on an inaccessible place, on a height; *vidhāvati*, flows —being dispersed becomes dissipated; *parvatesu*, over hills, over hilly lower regions; *evam*, similarly; *paśyan*, seeing; *dharmān*, the selves; *pṛthak*, differently—seeing It as different with respect to everybody; *anuvidhāvati*, one runs after; *tān eva*, them only—those souls that conform to the different bodies. The meaning is that he assumes different bodies again and again.

Now is being stated as to how the nature of the Self is attained by one who is a man of realization, for whom has been destroyed the perception of difference that is created by limiting adjuncts, who sees the non-dual Self which is a homogeneous mass of pure consciousness, and who is possessed of knowledge and is engaged in meditation:

यथोदकं शुद्धे शुद्धमासिक्तं तादृगेव भवति।
एवं मुनेर्विजानत आत्मा भवति गौतम ॥१५॥

इति काठकोपनिषदि द्वितीयाध्याये प्रथमा वल्ली ॥

15. O Gautama, as pure water poured on pure water becomes verily the same, so also does become the Self of the man of knowledge who is given to deliberation (on the Self).

Yathā, as; *śuddham udakam*, pure water; *āsiktam*, poured; *śuddhe*, on pure (water); *bhavati*, becomes; *tādṛk eva*, of that kind only, of the same quality and not anything else; *ātmā*, the Self , too; *bhavati*, becomes; *evam*, so; *vijānataḥ*, of one who knows—realizes unity; *muneḥ*, of one who deliberates, O Gautama. Therefore, giving up the perception of duality that bad logicians have and the erroneous notions that the non-believers entertain, the people whose pride has been quelled should eagerly seek after the realization of the unity of the Self, which is inculcated by the Vedas that are more beneficent than thousands of fathers and mothers. This is the idea.

PART II

Canto II

As Brahman is difficult to know, this is a fresh commencement for ascertaining in another way the reality that It is:

पुरमेकादशद्वारमजस्यावक्रचेतसः ।
अनुष्ठाय न शोचति विमुक्तश्च विमुच्यते । एतद्वै तत् ॥१॥

1. Of the unborn One, whose consciousness is unflickering, there is a city with eleven gates. Meditating (on Him), one does not grieve and, becoming freed, one becomes emancipated. This indeed is that.

Puram, a city, i.e. comparable to a city: the body is a city, since in it we find an assemblage of such appendages of a city as gate-keepers, their commanders, etc., and a city, together with its paraphernalia, is seen to be meant for an independent owner (viz the king) who is not a constituent part of it[1]; similarly, since this body, consisting of an assemblage of various paraphernalia, has resemblance to a city, it must exist for an owner who takes the position of a king, but does not form a part of it. This city then, that is called a body, *ekādaśadvāram*, is possessed of eleven doors—seven in the head, three, inclusive of

[1] He does not grow or contract even though the city may do so, and his existence can be known independently of the city.

the navel, in the lower parts, and one on the (top of the) head; because of these, it is a city possessed of eleven doors. Of whom? *Ajasya*, of the birthless One —of the Self which is free from all modifications, such as birth etc., which occupies the place of the king, and which is dissimilar to the properties of the city; *avakracetasaḥ*, of the One whose knowledge is not crooked—whose *cetaḥ*, consciousness; is *avakra*, straight, verily present for ever like the light of the sun—i.e. of Brahman which is comparable to the king. *Anuṣṭhāya*, by meditating—after becoming entirely free from desires—on Him to whom this city belongs, on the supreme Lord who is the owner of the city—for, his *anuṣṭhāna* (lit. performance) consists in contemplation with a view to complete knowledge[1]; by contemplating on Him as residing equally in all beings, *na śocati*, one does not grieve. How can there be any vision of fear, since there is no occasion for sorrow after the attainment of fearlessness resulting from His realization? Even here, (while still living), he becomes *vimuktaḥ*, free—free from the bondage of desire and duty, created by ignorance; *vimuktaḥ ca*, and having become free (while still living); *vimucyate*, he becomes emancipated, i.e. he does not take up a body again.

But He (the Self) does not reside in the city of one body only. What then? He exists in all the cities. How?

[1] Unobstructed, direct vision. Bālagopālendra interprets *samyagvijñānapūrvakam* as (meditation) that has complete realization as its objective.

हंसः शुचिषद्वसुरन्तरिक्षस-
द्धोता वेदिषदतिथिर्दुरोणसत्।
नृषद्वरसदृतसद्व्योमस-
दब्जा गोजा ऋतजा अद्रिजा ऋतं बृहत् ॥२॥

2. As the moving (sun) He dwells in heaven; (as air) He pervades all and dwells in the inter-space; as fire He resides on the earth; as Soma He stays in a jar; He lives among men; He lives among gods; He dwells in truth; He dwells in space; He is born in water; He takes birth from the earth; He is born in the sacrifice; He emerges from the mountains; He is unchanging; and He is great.

(As) *haṁsaḥ*, a mover—derived from the root *ham*, meaning to go; He is *śuciṣat*—derived from *śuci*, pure, and *sad*, to live—a dweller, as the sun, in heaven which is pure. *Vasuḥ* (air), derived from the causative form of the root *vas*, means 'one who provides a dwelling for all'. As air, He is *antarikṣasat*, a dweller in the intermediate space. As *hotā*, (meaning) fire—because of the Vedic text, 'Fire, indeed, is *hotā*' (Cit. III. 1, VII. 1); (He is) *vediṣat*—a resider (*sat*) on the *vedi*, the earth—because of the *mantra* which begins with, 'This *vedi* (sacrificial altar) is the highest state of the earth' (Ṛ. II. iii. 20). *Atithiḥ* (*san*), as the Soma juice; (He is) *duroṇasat*, a dweller in a jar (*duroṇa*); or as a Brāhmaṇa guest, He dwells in houses (*duroṇa*). (He is) *nṛṣat*, a dweller among men; *varasat*, a dweller among the adorable ones—the gods; *ṛtasat*, a dweller in *ṛta*, i.e. truth or sacrifice; *vyomasat*, a dweller in the *vyoma* (space); *abjāḥ*—derived from *ap* (water) and *jā* (to be born)—born in water, as conch, mother of pearl, *makara* (a sea animal), etc.; *gojāḥ*, born on earth (*go*), as paddy, barely, etc.; *ṛtajāḥ*, born in the sacrifice (*ṛta*), as its appendages; *adrijāḥ*, born from mountains (*adri*), as rivers etc.; although He is the Self of all, He is verily *ṛtam*, unchanging in nature; (and) *bṛhat*, great—being the cause of all. Even if it be a fact that the sun is spoken of in this verse (and not the Self), still, as the sun is regarded in reality as the Self, there is no contradiction with the *brāhmaṇa* which explains that way.[1] The meaning of this verse is that the world has but one Self which is all-pervasive, and that there is no plurality of selves.

A (logical) basis is being provided for comprehending the nature of the Self:

ऊर्ध्वं प्राणमुन्नयत्यपानं प्रत्यगस्यति ।
मध्ये वामनमासीनं विश्वे देवा उपासते ॥३॥

3. All deities worship that adorable One sitting in the middle, who pushes the *prāṇa* upward and impels the *apāna* inward.

The word *yaḥ*, he who, is to be supplied. He who

[1] 'In the *brāhmaṇa* portion of the Veda this verse is explained thus: "That sun is the *haṁsaḥ śuciṣat.*" But there is a *mantra* which says. "The sun is the Self of all that moves and does not move." (R. I. cxv. i; Ai. II. iii. 3) from which it is known that the sun symbolizes the all-pervasive Consciousness.'—A. G.

unnayati, leads higher up; *ūrdhvam*, upward—from the heart; *prāṇam*, the air functioning as exhalation; similarly, *pratyak asyati*, thrusts inward, downward; *apānam*, the air functioning as inhalation; that *vāmanam*, adorable One; *madhye āsīnam*, sitting in the middle—sitting in the space inside the lotus of the heart, shining in the intellect as revealed knowledge; *viśve*, all; *devāḥ*, deities—the organs such as the eye etc.; *upāsate*, worship—by carrying to Him presents in the form of perception of colour etc., just as the subjects do to a king. The idea is that they never cease from activity meant for Him. The purport of the sentence is that He for whom, and under whose direction, exist all the activities of the organs and the vital force, is proved to be different from them.

अस्य विस्रंसमानस्य शरीरस्थस्य देहिनः।
देहाद्विमुच्यमानस्य किमत्र परिशिष्यते। एतद्वै तत् ॥४॥

4. When this dweller in the body becomes detached, when He is freed from this body, what else remains here (in this body)? This indeed is that.

Moreover, *asya dehinaḥ śarīrasthasya*, of this embodied one (the Self) that is in the body; *visraṁsamānasya*, as It gets loosened, detached. The meaning of the word *visraṁsana* (loosening) is being given: *dehād vimucyamānasya*, as It gets freed from the body; *kim atra pariśiṣyate*, what else remains here—in this group of vital force etc.? Nothing remains here in this body. That Self is proved to be different (from the body etc.), on whose departure all this aggregate of body and senses becomes instantaneously powerless, defunct, and destroyed, just as it happens in the case of the citizens when the lord of the city retreats.

The opinion may be held that this body gets destroyed only on the departure of the *prāṇa*, *apāna*, etc., but not owing to the exit of the Self that is distinct from them; for a man lives only by *prāṇa* and the rest. But this is not so:

न प्राणेन नापानेन मर्त्यो जीवति कश्चन ।
इतरेण तु जीवन्ति यस्मिन्नेतावुपाश्रितौ ॥५॥

5. No mortal lives by *prāṇa* or *apāna*; but all live by something else due to which these two find asylum.

Na prāṇena na apānena, neither through the function of exhaling nor through that of inhaling—nor by the eye and the rest; *kaḥ cana martyaḥ*, any human being; *jīvati*, lives; nobody lives. Inasmuch as these are meant for somebody else and act jointly, they cannot be the source of life. Composite things like houses etc. are not seen to exist in this world, unless this existence is brought about by someone for his own benefit, who is not part of the assemblage. This should be so in the case of *prāṇa* etc. too, since they also form a combination. Therefore, all these *jīvanti*, live, maintain life, having been combined by someone else who is dissimilar to the *prāṇa* etc. which constitute the group. *Yasmin*, due to which—due to the existence of which supreme Self that is different from the combination; *etau*, these two—*prāṇa* and *apāna*, in combination with eye etc.; *upāśritau*, find asylum[1]; and for the benefit of which uncombined Self, *prāṇa*, *apāna*, etc. exist as a combination, performing their own functions—that Self is established to be distinct from them. This is the purport.

हन्त त इदं प्रवक्ष्यामि गुह्यं ब्रह्म सनातनम् ।
यथा च मरणं प्राप्य आत्मा भवति गौतम ॥६॥

6. Well, O Gautama, I shall tell you of this secret, eternal Brahman; and also how the Self fares after death.

Hanta, well, now again; *te*, to you; *pravakṣyāmi*, I shall tell; of *idam*, this; *guhyam*, secret; *sanātanam brahma*, everlasting Brahman; through the knowledge of which comes about a cessation of all worldly existence, and through the ignorance of which, *yathā*, how; *ātmā*, the soul; *bhavati*, fares, how it transmigrates; *maraṇam prāpya*, after death. That you hear, O Gautama.

योनिमन्ये प्रपद्यन्ते शरीरत्वाय देहिनः ।
स्थाणुमन्येऽनुसंयन्ति यथाकर्म यथाश्रुतम् ॥७॥

[1] Or, *yasmin* (*sati*), whose existence—the existence of which Self, supreme and distinct from the combination—being taken for granted; *etau upāśritau*, these two get supported.

7. Some souls enter the womb for acquiring bodies and others follow the motionless, in accordance with their work and in conformity with their knowledge.

Anye dehinaḥ, some souls, some embodied ones—some ignorant fools; *yonim prapadyante*, enter into the womb; *śarīratvāya*, for assuming bodies. *Anye*, others—the extremely inferior ones; after death, *anusaṁyanti*, follow; *sthāṇum*, the state of motionless things like trees etc.; *yathākarma*, in accordance as each one's work is—i.e. under the impulsion of the (fruits of) works they have accomplished in this life; similarly, too, *yathāśrutam*, in conformity with the nature of knowledge acquired. The idea is that they take bodies accordingly; for another Vedic text says: 'Creatures are born in accordance with their knowledge.'

The Upaniṣad speaks of the secret Brahman about which it was promised, 'I shall tell':

य एष सुप्तेषु जागर्ति कामं कामं पुरुषो निर्मिमाणः।
तदेव शुक्रं तद्ब्रह्म तदेवामृतमुच्यते।
तस्मिँल्लोकाः श्रिताः सर्वे तदु नात्येति कश्चन। एतद्वै तत् ॥८॥

8. That Puruṣa indeed, who keeps awake and goes on creating desirable things even when the senses fall asleep, is pure; and He is Brahman, and He is called the Immortal. All the worlds are fixed on Him; none can transcend Him. This indeed is that.

Yaḥ eṣaḥ, He who; *jāgarti*, keeps awake and does not sleep; *supteṣu*, when *prāṇa* etc. are asleep. How? *Nirmimāṇaḥ*, creating—through ignorance; *kāmam kāmam*, each of those desirable things—such desirable things as woman etc. *Puruṣaḥ*, the Puruṣa (all-pervading Brahman)—who keeps awake while accomplishing these; *tat eva*, that (Puruṣa) indeed; is *śukram*, white, pure; *tat brahma*, that is Brahman—there is no other secret Brahman. *Tat eva*, that indeed; *amṛtam ucyate*, is called the indestructible—in all the scriptures. Moreover, *sarve lokāḥ*, all the worlds—such as the earth etc.; *tasmin*, on It—on Brahman; *śritāḥ*, are supported—for It is the source of all the worlds. The text *tat u nātyeti kaścana* etc. is to be explained as before (in II. i. 9).

Since the knowledge of the unity of the Self, though validated by proof and reiterated more than once, does not find a lodging in the hearts of those Brāhmaṇas of insincere intellect, whose minds are swayed by the perverted intellect of numerous logicians, therefore the Upaniṣad, being eager to inculcate it, says again and again:

अग्निर्यथैको भुवनं प्रविष्टो
रूपं रूपं प्रतिरूपो बभूव ।
एकस्तथा सर्वभूतान्तरात्मा
रूपं रूपं प्रतिरूपो बहिश्च ॥९॥

9. Just as fire, though one, having entered the world, assumes separate forms in respect of different

shapes, similarly, the Self inside all beings, though one, assumes a form in respect of each shape; and (yet) It is outside.

Yathā, as; *agniḥ*, fire; though bright by nature and only *ekaḥ*, one; *praviṣṭaḥ*, having entered; *bhuvanam* — derived from the root *bhū* (to be), in the sense of a place where creatures come into being, the word means — this world; *rūpam rūpam prati*, in conformity with each form, i.e. in respect of the difference of combustible substances, such as wood etc.; *babhūva*, became; *pratirūpah*, multiformed, assuming the respective shapes of those different fuels; *tathā*, similarly; *sarvabhūtāntarātmā*, the Self that is inside all beings — by virtue of Its subtleness, like fire in fuels etc.; though only *ekaḥ*, one; has become *pratirūpaḥ*, formed in accordance with the individual shapes — in respect of all bodies, owing to Its entry there; *bahiḥ ca*, and (yet) It is outside — in Its own unmodified form, just like space.

Similarly there is another illustration:

वायुर्यथैको भुवनं प्रविष्टो
रूपं रूपं प्रतिरूपो बभूव ।
एकस्तथा सर्वभूतान्तरात्मा
रूपं रूपं प्रतिरूपो बहिश्च ॥१०॥

10. As air, though one, having entered into this world, assumes separate forms in respect of different shapes, similarly, the Self inside all beings, though

one, assumes a form in respect of each shape; and (yet) It is outside.

Yathā, as; *vāyuḥ*, air — in the form of vital force; having entered into the bodies; *rūpam rūpam prati-rūpaḥ babhūva* etc. is to be explained as before.

Since the contingency arises that if a single entity is the Self of all, then the sorrowfulness of the world will belong to the supreme Brahman Itself, (therefore) this is being said:

सूर्यो यथा सर्वलोकस्य चक्षु-
न र्लिप्यते चाक्षुषैर्बाह्यदोषैः।
एकस्तथा सर्वभूतान्तरात्मा
न लिप्यते लोकदुःखेन बाह्यः ॥११॥

11. Just as the sun, which is the eye of the whole world, is not tainted by the ocular and external defects, similarly, the Self, that is but one in all beings, is not tainted by the sorrows of the world, It being transcendental.

Yathā, as; *sūryaḥ*, the sun; even though by virtue of helping the eyes through its light, and illuminating such impure things as urine, ordure, etc., becomes *sarvalokasya cakṣuḥ*, the eye of all the people — who see those things; still *na lipyate*, it is not tainted; *cākṣuṣaiḥ bāhyadoṣaiḥ*, by the ocular and external blemishes — (by ocular faults), physical lapses amounting to sin, which are caused by the sight of impurity etc.; and by (external faults consisting in) the contact with impurity etc; *tathā*, similarly; (He who) though *ekaḥ*, one; is *sarvabhūtāntarātmā*, the Self inside all; *na lipyate lokaduḥkhena*, is not tainted by sorrows of the world; (since He is) *bāhyaḥ*, transcendental. For, it is through ignorance superimposed on the Self that people suffer the sorrows arising from desire and work. But that ignorance does not really inhere in one's Self just as the snake, the silver, the water, and the dirt, superimposed on a rope, a mother of pearl, a desert, and the sky (respectively), do not in reality exist as the distortions of the rope etc. But they appear as the defects of those things (rope etc.) because of the superimposition of false notions on the substances (rope etc.) that provide the bases for them.[1] They (the substances) are not tainted by those faults, for they are outside the notions thus falsely superimposed. Similarly, people, after having superimposed on the Self the false notions of actions, agent, and fruit, like that of a snake (on a rope), experience the misery of birth, death, etc., consequent on that superimposition; but the Self, though It is the Self of all, is not tainted by the sorrow of the world arising from false superimposition. Why? (Because It is) outside. For just like the rope etc., It is extraneous to the superimposition of false notion.

[1] Or, 'because of the superimposition of such false notions in the persons who come in contact with them.'

एको वशी सर्वभूतान्तरात्मा
एकं रूपं बहुधा यः करोति।
तमात्मस्थं येऽनुपश्यन्ति धीरा-
स्तेषां सुखं शाश्वतं नेतरेषाम् ॥१२॥

12. Eternal peace is for those—and not for others—who are discriminating and who realize in their hearts Him who—being one, the controller, and the inner Self of all—makes a single form multifarious.

Moreover, He indeed is the supreme Lord, all-pervasive, independent, and *ekaḥ*, one; there is none equal to or greater than Him. (He is) *vaśī*, the controller—for the whole universe is under His control. Why? Because (He is) *sarvabhūtāntarātmā*, the Self in all beings. *Ye dhīrāḥ*, those discriminating people who—those who have ceased from external activities; *anupaśyanti*, (who) realize directly—as a result of the pursuance of the instruction of the teacher—realize that God who is the Self; *yaḥ*, who, because of His inscrutable power; *karoti*, makes—by His mere existence; (His) *ekam rūpam*, one form—His own Self that is homogeneous and consists of unalloyed consciousness; *bahudhā*, diverse—through the differences in the impure conditions of name and form; (those who realize) *tam ātmastham*, Him as residing in the space of the heart within the body, i.e. as manifested as knowledge in the intellect, like a face appearing to exist in a mirror, it being impossible for the body to be the receptacle of the

Self that is formless like space; *teṣām*, for them, who have become identified with the supreme Lord; is *śāśvatam sukham*, eternal happiness—consisting in the blissfulness of the Self; *na itareṣām*, not for others, for those non-discriminating people whose intellects are attached to external things; because, though Bliss is their very Self, (they do not get it) owing to the obstruction of ignorance.

नित्योऽनित्यानां चेतनश्चेतनाना-
मेको बहूनां यो विदधाति कामान्।
तमात्मस्थं येऽनुपश्यन्ति धीरा-
स्तेषां शान्तिः शाश्वती नेतरेषाम् ॥१३॥

13. Eternal peace is for those—and not for others—who are discriminating and who realize in their hearts Him who—being the eternal among the ephemeral, the consciousness among the conscious—alone dispenses the desired objects to many.

Furthermore, (He is) *nityaḥ*, indestructible; *anityānām*, among the destructible; *cetanaḥ*, consciousness; *cetanānām*, among the conscious—among the manifestors of consciousness such as the living creatures beginning with Brahmā. As it is owing to fire that water etc., that are not fire, come to be possessed of the power to burn, similarly, the power to manifest consciousness that is seen in others is owing to the consciousness of the Self. Besides, He (is) the omniscient Lord of all—*yaḥ*, who; *ekaḥ*, alone; *vidadhāti*, ordains diversely, i.e. dispenses without effort;

kāmān, the desirable things—the fruits of work according to merit, as also enjoyable things out of His own grace; *bahūnām*, of many, of the desirous, worldly people. Those discriminating people who realize Him in their hearts—for them is *śāśvatī*, eternal; *śāntiḥ*, withdrawal—for them accrues peace that is their very Self; and *na itareṣām*, not for others who are of a different sort.

तदेतदिति मन्यन्तेऽनिर्देश्यं परमं सुखम् ।
कथं नु तद्विजानीयां किमु भाति विभाति वा ॥१४॥

14. How shall I know that supreme, unspeakable Bliss which they realize directly as 'This'? Is It self-effulgent—does It shine distinctly, or does It not?

(*Yat*) *tat*, that—that knowledge of the Self; that is *sukham*, bliss; *anirdeśyam*, indescribable; and *paramam*. superexcellent; (*yat tat*), that which, though beyond the range of speech and mind of ordinary people, still the Brāhmaṇas, who are free from desires, *manyante*, consider; *etat iti*, as 'This', as something directly known; *katham nu*, how indeed; *vijānīyām*, shall I know; *tat*, that—happiness; how can I make It an object of my consciousness as 'This', as do the *sannyāsins* who are free from desires? *Kim u tat bhāti*, does It shine?—That which is Self-effulgent, does It *vibhāti*, appear, is It seen, distinctly as an object of our intellect? *Vā*, or, is It not? (Or[1], since It is effulgent, is It perceived clearly as an object of our intellect, or is It not?)

[1] The word *yat* being interpreted as meaning *since*.

The answer to this (aforesaid question) is that It is both self-effulgent and shines distinctly (or multifariously). How?

न तत्र सूर्यो भाति न चन्द्रतारकं
नेमा विद्युतो भान्ति कुतोऽयमग्निः।
तमेव भान्तमनुभाति सर्वं
तस्य भासा सर्वमिदं विभाति ॥१५॥

इति काठकोपनिषदि द्वितीयाध्याये द्वितीया वल्ली ॥

15. There the sun does not shine, neither do the moon and the stars; nor do these flashes of lightning shine. How can this fire? He shining, all these shine; through his lustre all these are variously illumined.

Tatra, there—in Brahman which is one's Self; *sūryaḥ*, the sun; *na bhāti*, does not shine, i.e. it does not illuminate that Brahman, though it illumines all. Similarly, *na candratārakam*, *na imāḥ vidyutaḥ bhānti*, neither the moon and stars nor these flashes of lightning shine; *kutaḥ ayam agniḥ*, how can this fire—that is seen by us—(shine)? To cut short, all, inclusive of these, that shine, *anubhāti*, shine according as; *tam eva bhāntam*, He, the supreme Lord, shines. Just as (hot) water, fire-brand, etc., owing to their contact with fire, burn according as the fire does, but not independently, similarly, it is verily *tasya bhāsā*, by His effulgence; that *sarvam idam*, all this—the sun etc.; *vibhāti*, shine variously. This being so, it is that Brahman Itself that is effulgent and shines variously. Through the various kinds of effulgence in the effects, it is known that the characteristic of luminosity is intrinsic to that Brahman. Indeed, that which does not have intrinsic luminosity cannot impart it to others; for a pot etc. are not seen to illuminate others, whereas luminous things like the sun etc. are seen to do so.

PART II

Canto III

As in the world the root of a (silk-cotton) tree can be traced by coming to know its cotton,[1] similarly the sixth canto is commenced in order to ascertain the real nature of Brahman through the determination of the tree which is the effect that the world is, of which Brahman is the root:

ऊर्ध्वमूलोऽवाक्शाख एषोऽश्वत्थः सनातनः।
तदेव शुक्रं तद्ब्रह्म तदेवामृतमुच्यते।
तस्मिँल्लोकाः श्रिताः सर्वे तदु नात्येति कश्चन। एतद्वै तत् ॥१॥

1. This is the beginningless peepul tree that has its roots above and branches down. That (which is its root) is pure, that is Brahman and that is called immortal. On that are fixed all the worlds; none transcends that. This verily is that.

Ūrdhvamūlaḥ, that which has its roots above—the root that is the state of supreme Viṣṇu. This tree of the world, comprising everything from the Unmanifested to the immovables, has its root above. It is called *vṛkṣa* (tree) because (of the root-meaning)

[1] By seeing the cotton of the silk-cotton tree etc. one can infer that it comes from a tree which, though unseen, is rooted somewhere. Similarly, since the effect, the world, is seen, therefore its cause, Brahman, though unseen, must be there.

of being felled. It consists of many evils, such as birth, old age, death, sorrow, etc.; it changes itself every moment, inasmuch as no sooner is it seen than its nature is destroyed like magic, water in a mirage, a city in the sky, etc., and it ceases to exist ultimately like a tree; it is without any heart-wood like the stem of a plantain tree; it is subject to hundreds of doubts in the minds of sceptics; its reality is determined in its true colour by the seekers of truth[1]; its essence lies in its root, the supreme Brahman, ascertained in Vedānta; it grows from out of the seed of ignorance,[2] desire, action, and the Unmanifested; it has for its sprout Hiraṇyagarbha, the inferior Brahman, comprising the two powers of knowledge and action; it has for its trunk the diverse subtle bodies of all creatures; its vigour of growth results from the sprinkling of the water of desire; it has for its tender sprouts the objects of the senses of knowledge; its leaves are the Vedas, the Smṛtis, logic, learning, and instruction; its lovely flowers are the many deeds such as sacrifice, charity, austerity, etc.; its various tastes are the experience of happiness and sorrow; its innumerable fruits are the means of subsistence of beings; it has its secondary roots well developed, entwined, and firmly fixed through the sprinkling of the water of desire (for those fruits)[3]; it has for its

[1] Or, according to another reading, 'Its nature cannot be fixed as such and such by the seekers of truth.'

[2] Superimposition.

[3] Desires for works develop from desires for results; they get entwined and mixed up with various dispositions—*sāttvika*, *rājasika*, and *tāmasika* (calm, active, and lazy).

nests the seven worlds beginning from the one called Satya, built by the birds which are the living beings from Brahmā downwards; it has its uproar, rendered tumultuous through the various sounds arising from dancing, singing, instrumental music, disport (play, jest, etc.), clapping on the arms, laughing, pulling, crying, exclaiming 'Alas, alas!', 'Leave me, leave me!', induced by mirth and grief arising from the enjoyment and pain of living beings; and it is felled by the weapon of detachment consisting of the realization of the identity of Brahman and the Self as inculcated by Vedānta. This tree of the world is an *aśvatthaḥ*[1]—its nature is ever unsteady, like the peepul tree, shaken as it is by the wind of desire and deeds; it is *avākśākhaḥ*—downwards are its branches, consisting of heaven, hell, and states of beasts and ghosts; (it is) *sanātanaḥ*, existing from time immemorial, having no beginning. *Tat eva*, that very thing—which is the root of the tree of the world—is; *śukram*, white, pure, resplendent—being in reality the light of the Self which is Consciousness; *tat brahma*, that, indeed, is Brahman, being the greatest of all; *tat eva*, that indeed; *ucyate*, is called; *amṛtam*, indestructible by nature, being true. All else is false, being 'mutable, existing as mere name dependent on speech' (Ch. VI. i. 4), and hence it is mortal. *Tasmin*, on him, on Brahman that is absolutely true; *sarve*, all; *lokāḥ*, the worlds—which are comparable to a city in the sky, or water in a mirage, or jugglery, and which vanish on the realization of the supreme Truth;

[1] Lit. *a*, not; *sthātā*, existing; *śvas*, tomorrow; impermanent.

śritāḥ, are fixed—during creation, existence, and dissolution. *Kaḥ cana na*, nothing whatsoever—no modification; *atyeti*, transcends; *tat u*, that—that Brahman; just as the products like pot etc. do not transcend (their material) earth etc. This verily is that.

It may be said that the very root of the world, Brahman, by realizing which it is stated that people become immortal, does not exist, and that this (universe) has emerged out of nothing. But this is wrong:

यदिदं किं च जगत् सर्वं प्राण एजति निःसृतम् ।
महद्भयं वज्रमुद्यतं य एतद्विदुरमृतास्ते भवन्ति ॥२॥

2. All this universe that there is, emerges and moves because there is the supreme Brahman which is a great terror like an uplifted thunderbolt. Those who know this become immortal.

Prāṇe (*sati*), the supreme Brahman[1] (being there); *yat idam kim ca jagat sarvam*, all this universe that there is; *niḥsṛtam* (*sat*), having emerged; *ejati*, moves—acts regularly. That Brahman which is thus the cause of the origination etc. of the world is *mahat bhayam*, greatly terrifying—*bhayam* being derived in the sense of that from which one gets fear; *vajram udyatam*, like an upraised thunderbolt. The idea

[1] 'Brahman, being the source of activity of even the vital force (*prāṇa*), is figuratively referred to by the word *prāṇa*'—A.G.

imparted is that just as servants, finding their master in front with an uplifted thunderbolt, methodically follow his command, similarly this universe consisting of the sun, the moon, the planets, the constellations, and the stars, continues methodically without even a moment's respite because it has a God. *Ye*, those who; *viduḥ etat*, know this—the Brahman as the witness of all the activities of their minds; *te*, they; *bhavanti*, become; *amṛtāḥ*, possessed of deathlessness.

The text says how out of fear of Him the world behaves:

भयादस्याग्निस्तपति भयात्तपति सूर्यः ।
भयादिन्द्रश्च वायुश्च मृत्युर्धावति पञ्चमः ॥३॥

3. From fear of Him Fire burns, from fear shines the Sun; from fear run Indra and Air, and Death, the fifth.[1]

Bhayāt, from fear; (*asya*, of Him)—of the supreme Lord; *agniḥ tapati*, Fire burns; *bhayāt*, from fear; *tapati*, shines; *sūryaḥ*, the Sun; *bhayāt indraḥ*, from fear, Indra; *ca*, and; *vāyuḥ*, Air; *mṛtyuḥ ca*, and Death; *pañcamaḥ*, the fifth; *dhāvati*, runs. For unless there was a ruler, like one with an uplifted thunderbolt in hand, over these protectors of the world who themselves are lordly and powerful, there would not have been any regulated activity as that of servants trembling out of fear for their master.

[1] Fire etc. stand for their respective deities.

इह चेदशकद्बोद्धुं प्राक्शरीरस्य विस्रसः ।
ततः सर्गेषु लोकेषु शरीरत्वाय कल्पते ॥४॥

4. If one succeeds in realizing here before the falling of the body, (one becomes freed); (else) because of that (failure) one becomes fit for embodiment in the worlds of creatures.

Cet, if; (one) being competent; *aśakat*, i.e. *śaknoti*, succeeds; *boddhum*, in knowing—knows that Brahman which is the cause of this fear; even *iha*, here—while still living; *prāk śarīrasya visrasaḥ*, before the disintegration, falling off, of the body; then one becomes free from the bondage of the world. If one does not succeed in knowing, then *tataḥ*, because of that non-realization; *sargeṣu lokeṣu*, in the worlds of creatable things—on earth etc., the word *sarga* being derived from the root *sṛj*, in the sense of the places where creatable beings are created; *kalpate*, one becomes fit; *śarīratvāya*, for embodiment; the idea is that one assumes a body (in those worlds).

Hence effort is to be made for the realization of the Self before the falling off of the body, for here alone it is possible for the vision of the Self to be as clear as that of a face in a mirror, whereas this is not possible in other worlds apart from that of Brahmā, which however, is difficult to attain. How? This is being answered:

यथाऽऽदर्शे तथाऽऽत्मनि यथा स्वप्ने तथा पितृलोके ।
यथाऽप्सु परीव ददृशे तथा गन्धर्वलोके
छायातपयोरिव ब्रह्मलोके ॥५॥

5. As (one sees) in a mirror, so in one's intellect; as in a dream, so in the world of the manes; as it is seen in water, so in the world of the Gandharvas. As it is in the case of shade and light, so in the world of Brahmā.

Yathā, as—as one sees oneself very distinctly reflected; *ādarśe*, in a mirror; *tathā*, similarly; here *ātmani*, in one's own intellect—the idea is that, when the intellect has become spotless like a mirror, there springs a distinct vision of the Self. *Yathā svapne*, as in a dream—the vision arising from the impressions of the waking state is indistinct; *tathā*, similarly; indistinct is the vision of the Self *pitṛloke*, in the world of the manes—because of being entangled in the enjoyment of the results of work. *Yathā apsu*, as in water; one's form *pari iva dadṛśe*—is equivalent to *paridṛśyate iva*—appears to be without clear demarcation of the parts (hazy); *tathā*, similarly; indistinct is the vision of the Self *gandharvaloke*, in the world of the Gandharvas. It is known from the authority of the scriptures that similar is the case in other worlds as well. Only in one, viz *brahmaloke*, in the world of Brahmā, is the vision very distinct; *chāyā-ātapayoḥ iva*, as (it is) in the case of shade and light. But that world is difficult to attain, being the result of many special kinds of work and knowledge (i.e. of rites and meditation). Therefore, efforts should be made for the realization of the Self here itself. This is the idea.

How is He to be known and what is the need of His knowledge? This is being answered:

इन्द्रियाणां पृथग्भावमुदयास्तमयौ च यत्।
पृथगुत्पद्यमानानां मत्वा धीरो न शोचति ॥६॥

6. Having known the dissimilarity of the senses that originate separately, as also their rising and setting, the intelligent man does not grieve.

Indriyāṇām, of the senses—such as ear etc.; *pṛthak utpadyamānānām*, that are separately produced—from their sources, *ākāśa* etc., for the purpose of perceiving their own respective objects; *matvā*, knowing—through discrimination; their *pṛthagbhāvam*, difference—their nature of being essentially dissimilar to the nature of the Self that is extremely pure, absolute, and consciousness alone; similarly (knowing their) *udayāstamayau*, (rising and setting) creation and dissolution—in relation to the waking and sleeping states—as belonging to them only and not to the Self; *dhīraḥ*, the intelligent man; *na śocati*, does not grieve; for the constantly uniform nature of the Self being unchangeable, the Self cannot be the cause of sorrow. Similar is another Vedic text: 'The knower of the Self crosses over sorrow.' (Ch. VII. i.3)

The Self, in relation to which the dissimilarity of the senses has been pointed out, is not to be realized outside, for It is the inmost Self of all. How can that be? This is being said:

इन्द्रियेभ्यः परं मनो मनसः सत्त्वमुत्तमम्।
सत्त्वादधि महानात्मा महतोऽव्यक्तमुत्तमम् ॥७॥

7. The mind is superior to the organs; the intellect is superior to the mind; Mahat (the Great Soul) is superior to the intellect; the Unmanifested is superior to Mahat.

The sense-objects, belonging to the same class as the senses, are understood to be enumerated by the mention of the senses. The rest is as before (in I. iii. 10). By the word *sattva*, the intellect is referred to here.

अव्यक्तात्तु परः पुरुषो व्यापकोऽलिङ्ग एव च।
यं ज्ञात्वा मुच्यते जन्तुरमृतत्वं च गच्छति ॥८॥

8. But superior to the Unmanifested is the Puruṣa who is pervasive and is, indeed, without worldly attributes, knowing whom a man becomes freed and attains immortality.

Avyaktāt tu paraḥ, the Puruṣa is superior to the Unmanifested; and He is *vyāpakaḥ*, pervasive—for He is the source even of all pervasive things such as space etc.; *aliṅgaḥ*—*liṅga*, derivatively means that sign through which anything is comprehended, i.e. intellect etc.—He who has not that *liṅga*, intellect etc., is indeed *aliṅgaḥ*; that is, He is devoid of all worldly attributes; *eva*, indeed. *Yam jñātvā*, having known whom—from the teacher and the scriptures; *jantuḥ*, a man; *mucyate*, becomes freed—even while living—from the bondages of the heart, such as ignorance etc.; and when the body falls, he *gacchati amṛtatvam ca*, attains immortality as well. This part is to be construed with the earlier thus: He, the *aliṅgaḥ* (incomprehensible) Puruṣa, by knowing whom a man becomes free and attains immortality, is superior to the Unmanifested.

How can there, then, be any possibility of the vision of the incomprehensible? This is being said:

न संदृशे तिष्ठति रूपमस्य
न चक्षुषा पश्यति कश्चनैनम् ।
हृदा मनीषा मनसाऽभिक्लृप्तो
य एतद्विदुरमृतास्ते भवन्ति ॥९॥

9. His form does not exist within the range of vision; nobody sees Him with the eye. When this Self is revealed through deliberation, It is realized by the intellect, the ruler of the mind,[1] that resides in the heart. Those who know this become immortal.

Asya rūpam, His form—the form of this inmost Self; *na tiṣṭhati*, does not exist; *saṁdṛśe*, as an object of vision. Therefore, *na kaḥ cana*, nobody; *paśyati*, sees, perceives; *enam*, this Self—that is being considered; *cakṣuṣā*, through the eyes—i.e. through any of the senses, for the word *cakṣuḥ* (eye) is used

[1] The intellect is the ruler dissuading the mind from its occupation with objects. The identity of the Self and Brahman taught in the Upaniṣads, is confirmed by *manana*, deliberation. Then in the pure intellect, unoccupied with objects, arises the conviction, 'I am Brahman' from the Upaniṣadic text, 'That thou art.' Brahman becomes fully revealed to that convinced intellect.

here suggestively for all the senses. How, then, He is to be seen is being said: *hṛdā*, by that which is in the heart; *manīṣā*, by the intellect—*manīṭ* being that which, as the controller, rules (*īṣṭe*) the mind (*manas*) characterized by thought. *Abhiklṛptaḥ*, when (It is) confirmed, i.e. revealed; by that (intellect), the ruler of the mind, which is in the heart and is free from occupation with objects; *manasā*, through the adequate vision consisting in deliberation; then 'the Self can be realized'—this should be supplied to complete the sentence. *Ye*, those who; *viduḥ*, know; *etat*, this, this fact that the Self is Brahman; *te*, they; *amṛtāḥ bhavanti*, become immortal.

How can the ruler in the heart be attained? For that purpose yoga is being inculcated:

यदा पञ्चावतिष्ठन्ते ज्ञानानि मनसा सह ।
बुद्धिश्च न विचेष्टते तामाहुः परमां गतिम् ॥१०॥

10. When the five senses of knowledge come to rest together with the mind, and the intellect, too, does not function, that state they call the highest.[1]

Yadā, at the time when; *pañca jñānāni*, the five senses of knowledge—such as ear etc., which are called *jñāna* (knowledge), being meant for it; *saha manasā*, together with the mind, which the senses follow—together with the internal organ (mind)

[1] The state of yoga is called the highest because it leads to the highest goal.

which is (now) weaned away from (its functions of) thiṇking etc.; *avatiṣṭhante*, are at rest—in the Self alone, after desisting from their objects; *ca buddhiḥ*, and the intellect—characterized by determination; *na viceṣṭate*,[1] does not engage in its own activities; *tām*, that (state); *āhuḥ*, they call; *paramām gatim*, the highest state.

तां योगमिति मन्यन्ते स्थिरामिन्द्रियधारणाम् ।
अप्रमत्तस्तदा भवति योगो हि प्रभवाप्ययौ ॥११॥

11. They consider that keeping of the senses steady as yoga. One becomes vigilant at that time, for yoga is subject to growth and decay.

Manyante, they consider; *tām*, that state—which is such; viz *sthirām indriyadhāraṇām*, the steady control of the senses, i.e. keeping the inner and outer organs steady; *yogam iti*, as yoga (joining)—though in reality it is disjunction, for this state of the yogi consists in the cessation of the contact with all evils, and in this state, indeed, is the Self established in Its own nature, free from the superimposition of ignorance. *Bhavati*, one becomes; *apramattaḥ*, unerring—ever careful about the concentration of mind; *tadā*, at that time—at the very time that one commences yoga, which meaning follows from the implication of the context; for when the intellect etc. cease to function, there can be no possibility of carelessness; therefore, the carefulness is enjoined even before the

[1] An alternative reading is *viceṣṭati*.

cessation of the activities of the intellect etc. Or, since unimpeded vigilance is possible only when the senses are kept steady, therefore it is stated, 'One becomes unerring at that time.' Why? *Yogaḥ hi prabhavāpyayau*, for yoga is subject to growth and decay — this is the meaning. Therefore, vigilance is needed for avoiding decay.[1] This is the idea.

If Brahman be an object of the activities of the intellect etc., then It should be specifically apprehended as 'This is such and such'; and since It cannot be perceived on the cessation of the intellect etc., there being then no instrument for cognition, Brahman should surely have no existence (then). It is a well-known fact in the world that a thing exists so long as it is within the range of an instrument of cognition, and the contrary one is non-existent. Hence yoga is useless; or Brahman is to be perceived as non-existing inasmuch as It cannot be cognized. This contingency having arisen, this is the reply:

नैव वाचा न मनसा प्राप्तुं शक्यो न चक्षुषा ।
अस्तीति ब्रुवतोऽन्यत्र कथं तदुपलभ्यते ॥१२॥

12. It cannot be attained through speech, nor through mind, nor through eye. How can It be known

[1] The sentence 'Therefore' etc., follows up the first interpretation, where the Upaniṣad gives an injunction about the need of vigilance, the word 'becomes' being transformed into 'should become'. The second interpretation, starting with 'Or, since' is a statement of fact.

to anyone apart from him who speaks of It as existing?

It is true that *na eva vācā*, neither through speech; *na manasā*, nor through mind; *na cakṣuṣā*, nor through eye; nor even through the other senses; *prāptum śakyaḥ*, can It be attained. This is the idea. Still though It is devoid of all attributes, It does exist, since It is known as the root of the universe; for the denial of effects presupposes some existence as their ultimate limit. Similarly, this effect (in the form of the universe) when traced back in an ascending order of subtleness, makes one apprised of the idea of existence as its ultimate resort. Even when the intellect is being attenuated through the sublation of objects, the intellect dissolves only as pregnant with a concept of existence. And reason, indeed, is the proof for us in ascertaining the real nature of the existent and the non-existent. If the world had no root, this creation would be filled with non-existence and would be perceived as non-existent. But in fact, this is not so; it is perceived as 'existing', just as a pot etc., produced from earth etc., are perceived as permeated with earth. Therefore the Self, the root of the universe, is to be realized as existing. Why? *Asti iti bruvataḥ*, apart from the faithful one who, following the scriptures, speaks of existence; *katham*, how; can *tat*, that Brahman; *upalabhyate*, be known; *anyatra*, anywhere else—in the one who holds the theory of non-existence, in the one who thinks perversely in this way: The root of the world, the Self, does not exist; this effect is causeless, and it gets dissolved into non-existence as its end'? The idea is that It is not perceived in any way.

अस्तीत्येवोपलब्धव्यस्तत्त्वभावेन चोभयोः ।
अस्तीत्येवोपलब्धस्य तत्त्वभावः प्रसीदति ॥१३॥

13. The Self is (first) to be realized as existing, and (then) as It really is. Of these two (aspects), the real nature of the Self that has been known as merely existing, becomes favourably disposed (for self-revelation).

Therefore, eschewing the devilish company of those who advance the theory of non-existence, *asti iti eva upalabdhavyaḥ*, the Self should be realized as existing (i.e. immanent in all)—as productive of effects in which existence inheres, and as having the intellect etc. as Its limiting adjuncts. But when the Self is devoid of all that and is not subject to changes —and effects do not exist apart from their cause, because of the Vedic text, 'All transformation has speech as its basis, and it is name only. Earth as such is the reality' (Ch. VI. i. 4)—then, of that unconditioned, attributeless Self that is free from becoming an object of such concepts as existence and non-existence; *tattvabhāvaḥ*, the true (transcendental) nature—(*bhavati*) is revealed. (*Tattvabhāvena*), in that (truly revealed) form too—'is the Self to be realized', this much is to be supplied. The sixth (genitive) case in *ubhayoh* is used to imply selection. *Ubhayoḥ*, of the two (aspects), again—of the conditioned and the unconditioned, of the aspects of immanence and transcendence; the *tattvabhāvaḥ*, the real (transcendental) aspect; *asti iti eva upalabdhasya*, of that very Self which was earlier realized as existing[1] (as immanent), i.e. which was known through the idea of existence called up by the limiting adjuncts that are themselves the effects of an existing entity; (that real aspect of that very Self) *prasīdati*, becomes favourably disposed for revealing Itself later on—i.e. to the man who had realized It earlier as existence; the real aspect being that from which all limiting adjuncts have vanished, which is different from the known and unknown, is non-dual by nature, and is ascertained by such Vedic text as, 'not this, not this' (Bṛ. II. iii. 6, III. ix. 26), 'not gross, not subtle, not short' (Bṛ. III. viii. 8), 'in the changeless, bodiless, inexpressible, unsupporting' (Tai. II. vii. 1), etc.

यदा सर्वे प्रमुच्यन्ते कामा येऽस्य हृदि श्रिताः।
अथ मर्त्योऽमृतो भवत्यत्र ब्रह्म समश्नुते ॥१४॥

14. When all desires clinging to one's heart fall off, then a mortal becomes immortal (and he) attains Brahman here.

Thus, of the man who has realized the supreme Reality, *yadā*, when; *sarve kāmāḥ*, all desires; *pramucyante*, fall off, are broken to pieces, owing to the absence of anything else to be desired; *ye*, the desires which; *hṛdi śritāḥ*, clung to the heart; *asya*,

[1] The Self which was inferred as existing from the fact of Its being the cause of all the effects that are perceived as existing.

of that man of knowledge, before his enlightenment—the intellect, and not the Self, being the seat of the desires, which fact is also supported by another Vedic text, 'desire, thought, (doubt, etc., all these are but the mind)' (Bṛ. I. v. 3); *atha*, then; he who was before enlightenment *martyaḥ*, mortal; *amṛtaḥ bhavati*, becomes immortal, after enlightenment—by virtue of the elimination of death constituted by ignorance, desire, and deeds; death, which causes departure, having been destroyed, there remains no possibility of departure, and hence *atra*, here itself; owing to the cessation of all bondage, like the blowing out of a lamp, *samaśnute brahma*, (he) attains Brahman, i.e. (he) becomes Brahman Itself.

When again will the desires be totally uprooted? This is being said:

यदा सर्वे प्रभिद्यन्ते हृदयस्येह ग्रन्थयः।
अथ मर्त्योऽमृतो भवत्येतावद्ध्यनुशासनम् ॥१५॥

15. When all the knots of the heart are destroyed, even while a man is alive, then a mortal becomes immortal. This much alone is the instruction (of all the Upaniṣads).

Yadā, when; *sarve granthayaḥ*, all the knots—i.e. all concepts arising from ignorance, that bind one fast like knots; *hṛdayasya*, of the intellect; *prabhidyante*, get shattered, are destroyed; *iha*, here—even while a man is living. The concepts arising from ignorance are, 'I am this body', 'This wealth is mine',

'I am happy and unhappy', etc. When the bondages of ignorance are destroyed by the rise of the opposite knowledge of the identity of the Self and Brahman, in the form, 'I am Brahman indeed, and am not a transmigrating soul', then the desires originating from the knots become totally eradicated. *Atha martyaḥ amṛtaḥ bhavati*, then a mortal becomes immortal. *Etāvat hi*, this much only is—there should not be any anticipation that there is more; *anuśāsanam*, the instruction; the expression, 'of all the Upaniṣads', should be supplied to complete the sentence.

By asserting 'He attains Brahman here' (II. iii. 14), it has been declared that there is no going for an enlightened man of whom all the knots of ignorance become destroyed on the realization of the identity of the Self with the all-pervading and absolutely attributeless Brahman, and who becomes Brahman even while living, which fact is also supported by another Vedic text: 'Of him the organs do not depart. Being but Brahman he is merged in Brahman.' (Bṛ. IV. iv. 6) But for those who are not much advanced in the knowledge of Brahman, who are engaged in other kinds of knowledge (i.e. in worship and meditation), and who are fit for the world of Brahmā, as also for those others who are the opposite of these and are fit for worldly existence, this particular kind of path is stated with a view to eulogizing the superior result of the knowledge of Brahman that is being treated here. Moreover, the knowledge of Fire had been questioned about and was imparted. The process of the attainment of the fruit of that knowledge has also to be described. Hence this verse is begun. As to that,

शतं चैका च हृदयस्य नाड्य-
स्तासां मूर्धानमभिनिःसृतैका ।
तयोर्ध्वमायन्नमृतत्वमेति
विष्वङ्ङन्या उत्क्रमणे भवन्ति ॥१६॥

16. The nerves of the heart are a hundred and one in number. Of them one passes through (the crown of) the head. Going up through that (nerve) one gets immortality. The others that have different directions, become the causes of death.

The nerves that issue out of the heart of a man are *śatam*, a hundred in number; *ca ekā*, and one—called *suṣumṇā*. *Tāsām*, of these; *ekā*, the one—the *suṣumṇā*; *abhiniḥsṛtā*, goes out; by piercing through *mūrdhānam*, (the crown of) the head. At the time of death one should bring one's mind under control through that (*suṣumṇā*) nerve, and get it concentrated in the heart. *Tayā*, through that nerve; *ūrdhvam āyan*, going up—along the Path of Sun (*uttara-mārga*); one *eti*, attains; *amṛtatvam*, immortality—which is relative because of the Smṛti, 'The place (i. e. Brahmaloka) that lasts till the absorption of all the elements (i. e. cosmic dissolution) is called immortality.' (V. P. II. viii. 97) Or, after having enjoyed incomparable pleasures abounding in the world of Brahmā, he attains immortality, in the primary sense of the word, along with Hiraṇyagarbha (Brahmā), in due course of time. *Viṣvak anyāḥ*, the other nerves that branch out (otherwise), in different directions; become the causes *utkramaṇe*, of death, i.e. for the attainment of the worldly state alone.

Now, with a view to concluding the purport of all the cantos the Upaniṣad says:

अङ्गुष्ठमात्रः पुरुषोऽन्तरात्मा
सदा जनानां हृदये संनिविष्टः ।
तं स्वाच्छरीरात्प्रवृहेन्मुञ्जादिवेषीकां धैर्येण ।
तं विद्याच्छुक्रममृतं तं विद्याच्छुक्रममृतमिति ॥१७॥

17. The Puruṣa, the indwelling Self, of the size of a thumb, is ever seated in the hearts of men. One should unerringly separate Him from one's body like a stalk from the Muñja grass. Him one should know as pure and immortal. Him one should know as pure and immortal.

Aṅguṣṭhamātraḥ puruṣaḥ antarātmā sadā janānām hṛdaye, in the heart as related to men; *saṁniviṣṭaḥ*—all this is as has been already explained (vide II. i. 12-13). *Tam*, Him; *pravṛhet*, one should raise, should pull out, i.e. should separate; *svāt śarīrāt*, from one's own body. Like what? That is being said: *Dhairyeṇa*, unerringly; *iṣīkām iva muñjāt*, like a stalk from the Muñja grass, that is inside it. *Vidyāt*, one should know; *tam*, that thing—the absolute Consciousness that has been separated from the body; to be *śukram amṛtam*, pure and immortal —to be the Brahman previously described. The repetition (of 'Him one should . . .', etc.), as also the word *iti*, is to show that the Upaniṣad is concluded.

Now this conclusion of the purport of the story is being stated with a view to eulogizing the knowledge:

मृत्युप्रोक्तां नचिकेतोऽथ लब्ध्वा
विद्यामेतां योगविधिं च कृत्स्नम् ।
ब्रह्मप्राप्तो विरजोऽभूद्विमृत्यु-
रन्योऽप्येवं यो विदध्यात्ममेव ॥१८॥

18. Naciketā, having first become free from virtue and vice, as also desire and ignorance, by acquiring this knowledge imparted by Death, as also the process of yoga in its totality, attained Brahman. Anyone else, too, who becomes a knower thus (like Naciketā) of the indwelling Self, (attains Brahman).

Naciketā, *labdhvā*, having attained—from Death, through the granting of boons; *mṛtyuproktām etām vidyām*, this knowledge of Brahman imparted by Death—as stated above; *yogavidhim ca kṛtsnam*, and the process of yoga in its entirety, i.e. together with all its accessories and results. What happened to him after that? *Brahmaprāptaḥ abhūt*, (he) attained Brahman, i.e. became free. How? By having already become *virajaḥ*, free from virtue and vice; (and) *vimṛtyuḥ*, free from desire and ignorance, through the acquisition of knowledge. Not only Naciketā, but *anyaḥ api*, anyone else, too — becomes like Naciketā (a knower of Brahman) by attaining the Self, existing in the context of the body, as one's own innermost reality in Its absoluteness, and not in any form other than as the indwelling Self. He who knows *adhyātmam eva*, the Self that exists in the context of the body — in the manner as described; who is an *evamvit*, a knower of this kind; 'he, too, having become *virajaḥ*, (free from virtue and vice); becomes *vimṛtyuḥ* (free from desire and ignorance)[1] — by knowing Brahman' — this (sentence) is to be added to complete the idea.

This valedictory prayer is uttered with a view to removing all faults incurred by the disciple and the teacher through lapses resulting from inadvertence during the course of acquiring or imparting the knowledge:

ॐ सह नाववतु । सह नौ भुनक्तु । सह वीर्यं करवावहै ।
तेजस्वि नावधीतमस्तु मा विद्विषावहै ॥१९॥
ॐ शान्तिः शान्तिः शान्तिः ॥

इति काठकोपनिषदि द्वितीयाध्याये तृतीया वल्ली ॥

19. May He protect us both (by revealing knowledge). May He protect us both (by vouchsafing the results of knowledge). May we attain vigour together. Let what we study be invigorating. May we not cavil at each other. *Om*! Peace! Peace! Peace!

[1] In this context some translate *vimṛtyuḥ* as 'immortal'.

Avatu, may He protect; *saha nau*, both of us together—by revealing the real nature of knowledge. Who? That supreme God Himself who is revealed in the Upaniṣads. Besides, *bhunaktu*, may He protect; *saha nau*, both of us together—by revealing the result of that knowledge. *Karavāvahai*, may we both accomplish; *saha*, together—jointly indeed; *vīryam*, the power—originating from knowledge. Moreover, let *adhītam*, the lesson; *tejasvinau* (is to be construed as *tejasvinoḥ*), of us two who are of sharp intellect (be befitting for us)—let what has been studied by us be well studied. Or the meaning is: Let *nau adhītam*, what has been studied by us two; be very *tejasvi*, potent, invigorating *Mā vidviṣāvahai*, may we two not cavil at each other—i. e. may we not entertain that antagonism subsisting between a disciple and his teacher owing to defects in study and teaching that originate from unwitting lapses. *Śānitiḥ*, *śāntiḥ*, *śāntiḥ*, peace, peace, peace—this repetition for three times is to avert all evils.[1] *Om*.

[1] On the three planes—physical, natural, and supernatural.

INDEX TO ŚLOKAS